MW00436495

HEBREW BOOK OF THE DEAD

IN THE WILDERNESS

Translation and Commentary
ZHENYA SENYAK

Tiktin Press, Hallandale, FL, 2003

The Hebrew Book of the Dead: *In the Wilderness*
Copyright© 2003 by Zhenya Senyak.
(Reflections of a Conservative Rabbi, © 2002 Jonathan P. Slater)

This edition of *The Hebrew Book of the Dead, In the Wilderness,* is published by arrangement with Tiktin Press. All rights reserved. No part of this book may be reproduced in any manner without written permission except for brief quotations in critical articles and reviews.

FIRST EDITION

ISBN 0-9717560-1-5

Published by Tiktin Press
1835 E. Hallandale Beach Blvd.
Hallandale, Florida 33009

http://www.tiktinpress.com

For inquiries contact the publisher or: orders@ipgbook.com
Distributor: Independent Publishers Group 800.888.4741

©Tiktin Press

לחנה

To Karen, my guardian angel.

הנה אנכי שלח מלאך לפניך לשמרך בדרך

Exodus 23:20

The Hebrew Book of the Dead

Contents

The Hebrew Book of the Dead

Acknowledgements

When the making of a book stretches across two decades, it is difficult to acknowledge fairly the many hands that went into its creation. Certainly, at the top of the list, should be Huston Smith, in whose Syracuse home I found the first books on mystical Judaism and the living inspiration that set me on this path. In the ensuing decades, his calm sweet wisdom and encouragement kept me at this task.

To my parents and children and grandchildren, I owe much of the sense of life and loss that permeates this book. Deeply loved and deeply grieved, their precious presence accompanies my soul all my days.

I am indebted to the many rabbis who taught me Hebrew and midrash and led me into the paths of Torah: Michael Starr in New York City; Martin Ballonoff of Berkeley, Joseph Leibowitz at Beth Israel in Berkeley, now in Kfar Saba; Emanuel Forman in Netanya; Aryeh Wineman, in Troy; and my close friend and mentor, Jonathan Slater, without whose example and erudition this book most surely would not have been completed. Chief among these rabbis stands my *zayde*, Rebbe Joseph Levenstein of Tiktin and Brooklyn, my first teacher.

Of my fellow seekers on the path, there are innumerable souls to acknowledge, including Baruch BenDetz, Danny Matt, Suzanne Sadowsky, David Skau, Shimon Neustein, Jon Batzdorff, Michael Shapiro, Bashi Davis, and Stephanie Onel, all of whom suffered endless questions, and shared visions and insights from the Torah. A special grateful acknowledgement is due Dakota Lane for her valiant editorial assistance and Judith Antonelli, my scrupulous copy editor. The errors that remain are entirely my own responsibility. For the many people I have omitted, may those I have named stand in their place.

In the spirit of *devekuth,* may this translation and commentary help lighten our way in the wilderness.

Clear a path for YHVH in the wilderness. במדבר פנו דרך יהוה

The Hebrew Book of the Dead

x

Foreword

The world is well acquainted with *The Egyptian Book of the Dead* and its successor, *The Tibetan Book of the Dead.* Now comes *The Hebrew Book of the Dead.*

The *Hebrew Book of the Dead* is the hidden esoteric message embedded in the Hexateuch, the first six books of the Hebrew Bible: its first five books — Genesis, Exodus, Leviticus, Numbers, and Deuteronomy, known as the Pentateuch or Torah — plus the Book of Joshua. The Hexateuch begins with the story of the creation of the world and human beings, and then turns its attention to the soul's journey on Earth and its eventual return to its Maker. It couches this account in a dramatic narrative which comes close to being the bedrock of Western civilization.

Every schoolchild knows the story of a people who were sold into slavery, miraculously set free, and endured great hardships before crossing a river to inherit a promised land. The people are the Israelites, their slavery is to the Egyptians, their miraculous deliverance is through the Red Sea. The ordeal they then face is forty years of wandering in a wilderness before they finally cross the Jordan River into a land of milk and honey.

Everyone with the slightest knowledge of how stories work can see how readily the storyline of this narrative can be transferred to the life of every human being; indeed, it is the fact that it lends itself so readily to this transfer that has given it its power. For we are all born with bodies and we all face ordeals which, if courageously dealt with, produce happy endings. This is the greatest masterplot conceivable, for if any of its components are omitted life is meaningless.

The originality of *The Hebrew Book of the Dead* lies in the way it shows that the applicability of the Hexateuch's storyline to individual souls is explicit in the Hexateuch itself. We do not have to extract that storyline from the accounts of wars, plagues, and the like and then apply it to our individual lives. If the Hebrew words are read aright (much has been lost in forgetfulness of the original, literal meaning of those words, to say nothing of the loss brought about in translations) we find the Hexateuch's real referent is the nature and destiny of the human soul as these truths body forth in a gripping segment of human history.

A daunting amount of detective work — historical, anthropological, and above all linguistic — has gone into the making of this thesis. Not knowing Hebrew myself, I am in no position to pronounce on its accuracy. What I can say is that to my eyes this is the most original addition to Biblical understanding that I have seen in my lifetime.

— *Huston Smith, Berkeley, California*

Introduction

For very near to you is the Word, in your mouth and in
your heart that you may do it. (Deuteronomy 30:13)

I came to Hebrew not as a student but as a traveler,
lost in a forest, who comes upon an obscure path
and follows it, twig by twig, stone by stone. Over the
course of many years reading the Hebrew Scriptures, I
came to understand the shape and rumbling of Hebrew words and discovered some that opened the way.
I carried those words to my teachers and compared
them in books and commentaries until my mind confirmed what my heart uncovered.

In the opening of the Book of Ezekiel, the
prophet writes of his vision of the Chariot.

Surrounded by brightness, in the midst of
the fire came the likeness of four living creatures. ...and out of the fire went forth lightning and the living creatures ran and returned at the sight of a *bazak* (a lightning
flash).

It is in the flash of lightning, the first splitting
apart of darkness by the electrifying bolts of light, the
bazak itself, that we experience revelation, sudden
understanding of a darkly obscured field. In *The Hebrew Book of the Dead* we hear much of the word
karov, meaning "near." Closer yet is the state in

which something is very near or *karov meod.* Lightning itself is illuminating, terrifying, powerful. But the flash of lightning brings us *karov meod* to the light, *karov meod* to understanding.

When I came to Hebrew Scripture, ignorant and innocent, all was fresh and new. Within the thicket of genealogy and cult, beyond stories that settle tribal scores and text that claims levitical rights, I found *The Hebrew Book of the Dead,* glinting flecks of gold, hidden by tracks of passage on a well-worn path through the dark forest. It had been there from the beginning. Each story, each section, each illumination on that path was a *bazak.*

At the conclusion of the Book of Job, God appears to Job out of the whirlwind and Job says, "I have heard of you with the hearing of the ear, but now my eye sees you and I repent in dust and ashes." He has been brought *karov meod* to the light. I have been to temples and synagogues, churches and meeting rooms in which, with a bow and a nod, God is acknowledged between breakfast and lunch. Thus, in our hearts and in our places of ritual worship, we draw a curtain over the terror, the awe and magnificence of Being in order to proceed in our sensory gratifications and fantastical illusions, blind and very far from the light.

Some teachers consider this book midrash, Torah interpretation. But for many others it is simply literal Hebrew Scripture, direct translation of the Word that has appeared in the Torah and the Book of Joshua for more than three thousand years. In reality, such categorization does not matter. Simply, from a literal perspective, *The Hebrew Book of the Dead* surely exists within this most ancient of Hebrew writings. Across all generations of telling, composition, and copying, it stands out in sharp relief from surrounding materials. Those who read *The Hebrew Book of the Dead* may come away from Hebrew Scripture with a fresh vision of the realities beneath its flaming letters and the landscape of the desert wanderings.

 The Hebrew Book of the Dead traces a human life from Creation, from the planting of a Tree of Life in the Garden of Eden to the planting of a Tree of Death in a cave in the Promised Land. The major portion of the book is set in the World of Yetzirah, the desert wilderness beyond the Sea of Ending, a world filled with Angels and trials, a World where the soul is prepared for reincarnation across the Sea of Descent. Each word is found in the Hebrew Torah and the Book of Joshua.

 Hebrew Scripture is the hidden deep spring that feeds the fountains of Western religion. These scrolls of the Ancient Hebrews are the ultimate sourcetext for the religious and spiritual life of the Western world, and yet they do not mention Christian or Jew or Moslem. Hebrew Scripture comes to us on its own terms but for millennia humanity has adopted it as its own, scarcely considering the Hebrew words at the root of its beliefs, the Hebrew visions at the heart of the words. This is the tent and humble clay house on which are built the soaring temples and cathedrals of Western civilization.

When I finally emerged from the forest, I found there were forty-four *bazakim*, a few hundred lines of text, that revealed this ancient vision. There are likely other *bazakim*, but these, at least, are certain.

This volume of commentary on *the Hebrew Book of the Dead* is sub-titled, *In the Wilderness*. (That sub-title is the literal translation of *bamidbar*, the portion of the Torah called, in English, the Book of Numbers.) *In the Wilderness* contains the twelve principal *bazakim,* the sections that trace the outlines of the cosmic journey from Creation through birth, death, purification, renewal and reincarnation. In addition to those twelve *bazakim*, this edition includes summaries of the other thirty-two identified *bazakim*.

Throughout the *Hebrew Book of the Dead* runs a common thread: To perceive the God of Being, it is necessary to be in the present streaming moment, necessary to get *karov meod* to the onrushing of time. For it is only there, at that *bazak* of an intersection, that we come alive to witness and participate in Creation. No looking away. No looking back.

In the present moment, the breath in our mouth and the beat of our heart reveals itself as the Word of God. In the present moment we feel most deeply that God is truly with us.

The landscape of *The Hebrew Book of the Dead* extends from the first instant of Creation and brings us beyond the Gates of Death. It is an ancient vision that speaks to the essential nature of our life as beings of mud inhabited briefly by an immortal Divine spirit. It is a searing vision that leads to freedom and deep attachment to God.

There is a path through the Hebrew Scripture, a way through the tangle of myth and genealogy, of curses and cult. There is a shining path through the wilderness laid out, from beginning to end, in simple words. Hebrew words. Each *bazak* is a step on that path, and each follows the other on up from light to light, from life to life, from World to World. Nothing need be taken on faith for this is the Torah of the Ancient Hebrews and it speaks to our own experience today as it did in the time of the revelations.

It is only right now, in the present streaming moment, that we are alive or dead, transcendent or gross, mud person or Divine. At all times we have the choice to turn our hearts to God, to be free to cling to the Tree of Life in devotion, in *devekuth*. So too do we have the choice to turn away and follow our greeds and impulses, idly click through TV channels or make of our hours a practical, duty-bound round of errands and deadlines, hopes and fears, lists and exhaustions.

We can choose life or we can choose death in each moment. In fact, we do.

It is that awareness of time and the burning fragility and promise of life in each moment that eternally links us to this ancient Hebrew vision.

Come and see.

A Mystical Journey through the Worlds

Looking out at the limitless expanse of a dark, clear night we are aware, as were our earliest ancestors, of the worlds stretching beyond our vision. We sense no wind as we speed along on our thousand-mile-per-hour twirling Earth, no turbulence in our elliptical journey around our faithful Sun, no creaking of planets in their orbits beyond our hearing.

And yet we do twirl and speed, roar and creak. Amid the trillions of star filled galaxies exploding away from us in every direction, in silent cacaphony we dance a carousel dance around the sun. In a universe filled with dark matter and dark energy, we are seldom aware we live in worlds wrapped within worlds, following the course of a life wrapped in a dark and flaming mystery.

While we follow the daily path of our earthly life, oblivious on our green blue fecund planet to blazing supernovas and collapsing universes light centuries away, we know there is another dimension beyond this sensual life, a reality somehow related to those infinitely distant worlds. Although stars we see in deep space have long since vanished, we sense we are joined. This universe is our home. We are part of the shower of stardust, children of light in the absolute zero of a dark universe.

As above, so below. The infinity of endless space is reflected in the infinitudes of sub-atomic particles whirling in and through miniature universes far below the penetrations of our deepest instruments. Where once we suspected molecules and atoms, today we measure quarks, muons, and neutrinos interpenetrating all matter in blazing trillions of multitudes. Are these too not worlds?

There are deeper Worlds surrounding, supporting, dictating the logic of all these invisible infinities, spiritual Worlds from which they derive, Worlds that have been all but lost to us in the technological hubris of the past century.

While our science and mathematics, electron microscopes, computers, space satellites and spectrometers have extended the reach of our minds, we have paid a heavy price by contracting the reach of our hearts. For in our antiquities there were gods and demons, heros, archangels, and the supreme Creator. Today, by and large, we are turned from the bright and magical flashes of insight into the soul by the eleven o'clock news and the nattering compulsion of our technologies.

Faced by death or some other transforming event, the nature of this strange journey is brought home to us. The fundamental reality, the underlying cause and meaning of this life into which we are born naked, blind, and bloody is hidden from us by the glitter of our accomplishments, the shadow of our fears, the dullness of our senses. When confronted by the abyss of endless possibility, we most need to tear the wrappings away from the hidden face of the universe. We need to meet the Intelligence informing the universe, the Creator who set in motion this explosion of light and continually unfolding life.

It is not beyond the constraints of our diminished hearts to consider all these hidden universes, all the awesome forces of nature, as manifestations of God moving through the Worlds. It is a reasonable hypothesis. But there is another leap, a further and far more risky consideration: What if God not only moves through the world but actually engages us, loves us, continually? Physically, we are entered into a covenantal relationship with God that is transcribed in our DNA, confirmed in each breath and each heartbeat, a relationship direct and responsible, a living and demanding relationship.

This streaming, speeding, exploding Universe, this great gob of galaxies, then takes on a different coloring, no longer dark in the absolute zero of space but home, a universe wearing not an opaque nor demonic but a Divine face.

Amid the joys and heartless horrors of daily life on this insignificant molecule of rock and water, where is the promise of God's love, what message has been given to us that the Intelligence brooding over all the universe holds us dear to its heart?

One of humanity's most ancient series of documents not only lays claim to be a record of God's love for Creation but, until our own raucous modern times, had bent much of human history to its world view.

The Natural World of the Spirit

To believe today that the Torah of the Hebrews, a revelation made to a straggling collective of frequently warring Semitic tribes, a scroll replete with inconceivable and often self-serving claims, contains a holy and accurate view of this hidden spiritual world does not require a leap of faith. It requires direct experience.

Once experienced, once the path is made clear, the mountains lowered and the valleys raised, the very center

of spiritual life is altered. We realize God has been moving in our hearts and in our world, demanding a living,
constant response from us. Often these realizations occur
at breakthrough instants. The moment of death. A birth
or car accident. Sudden joy, sudden sorrow reveal the reality that was always there, dodging our footsteps, all the
way along the path, urging us to look up out of our mud
bodies and see. And be.

We are required to live with quiet vigilance to witness
the stream of BE-ing in which we flow. Quiet centered
watchfulness is commanded in the Hebrew Scripture.
"Choose life that you may live to love the Lord" is a
choice that is made each living instant, a choice demanding that we be awake. For the real Covenant, the gift beyond all value, is the nearness of God, witnessed by the
breath in our mouth, the heart beating in our breast.
"For very near to you is the Word, in your mouth and in
your heart, that you may do it."

When all reason fails, in all seasons of distress, these
words have the power to bring us back to the moment,
breath by breath, beat by beat, and become still so we can
hear the Word. This Word is our heart's companion. It
calls us to action. It calls us home.

There are many roads to experience knowing God,
however briefly, however partially. *The Hebrew Book of
the Dead* is a path that winds deep within the ancient Hebrew Scripture, a path filled with glory, rich with years
and richer in tears. Discovering the golden thread in the
stories of the Torah, and following it as the Hebrew
Worlds and the mysteries of the *Sephirot* (please see Appendix C) slowly open, leads us along the way of the wil-

derness, the desert path to the waters leading to the Promised Land.

For the traveler on this path, it is as if a great weight has been laid down. The journey continues, only now it has moved from the World of Nature to the natural World of the Spirit. In the Kabbalah, these Worlds have names. The World of Nature is the world of space and time, gravity and pride. It is the world in which we are embodied and the world in which we leave our body. When we are born nothing is added to this World and when we die nothing is taken from this World. For this is the World of Assiyah, the World of Doing and Making.

Another World, encompassing this one, is more luminous and, in its way, more limited. It is Yetzirah, the World of Formation. It is here that the naked soul is formed and the delusions of the flesh are cleared so that the reflected glory and light of God can again be experienced. It is in Yetzirah that the soul is prepared for incarnation and returned to the World of Assiyah to do the work of God

Descriptions and messages from this World of the Spirit make up much of the Hexateuch. (The whole Book of Genesis may be read as a long prologue to the events of the wilderness, a vestibule to the World of Yetzirah.) For these ancient Hebrew scribes and priests seized on their revelations to record incandescent days of mystery and promise in a manual that became a Tree of Life to this very day. Beyond the purely tribal and cultic, but sharing in that language and world, the Hexateuch describes the passage of a human soul from death to rebirth within the body of God, the very same journey we each make in our lives.

The assertion that God loves and guides us is both heartening and staggering in these cynical and deeply materialistic times. *The Hebrew Book of the Dead* reveals God's love drifting as light through the universes not only into the exultant heart of a wandering tribe but into all human consciousness, all sentient beings. Preserving, protecting, redeeming. To feel the joy and blessings of this love requires a human response, *devekuth*, wholehearted cleaving to God. It is the final commandment of the Torah.

The Hebrew words of Scripture are hewn of light and drawn from the very heart of Creation. They reflect an awesome revelation deeply hidden in the Torah.

The Hero's Quest

To read the *peshat* or simple narrative of *The Hebrew Book of the Dead* is to enter upon a classical story of the hero's quest. The object of the quest is to bring the blessings of the Covenant of the Lord of the Universe across the Worlds, beyond the grave, in order to be reborn in the Promised Land after facing the trials of the desert wilderness.

Joseph, called Asaph, the Carried Off, is the bearer of the blessing passed on in the covenant between his fathers and God. (The origin of his name comes from the Book of Genesis, 30:23. Rachel bore a son and said "God has taken away (*Asaph*) my reproach.) He is given the gift of prophetic dreams. This gift leads to his early downfall and later helps him rise to enormous power in Egypt. Asaph dies after exacting a promise from his kinsmen that his bones will be brought up from Egypt and carried across to the Promised Land to fulfil the covenant.

Four hundred years later the final quest begins. The children of Israel are now persecuted and laboring as slaves, To become free, they must escape bondage to a tyrannical Pharaoh and cross the *Yam Sof,* the Sea of Ending, carrying with them the bones of Asaph. With the help of a powerful Angel, Mosheh the Bearer, the children of Israel cross the waters, confront their slavish impulses, and experience revelation and redemption in the *midbar,* the desert wilderness.

The cycle of transformation is completed when the children of Israel bury the bones of Asaph in the ground of the Promised Land, placing the seed of the patriarchs in that land promised to Abraham, Isaac, and Israel by the Lord of the Universe.

The hidden Worlds

The *sod,* or hidden meaning, behind this narrative operates on many levels, using mythic universal human symbols like the waters of unconsciousness, sacrificial fire, transformation and agricultural rites. Deeper meanings rely on a uniquely Hebrew concept of Worlds.

At the heart of Jewish mysticism, within teachings of Kabbalah, there is a hierarchy of Worlds, alluded to in early literature like the *Sefer Yetzirah* (the Book of Formation) and the *Bahir* (Brilliance). These Worlds, deriving from the *Ayn Sof,* the Eternal One, reflect each other, derive from each other in the unfolding emanation of Creation. (See Appendix C, "On Worlds and the Sephirot.")

In *Aytz Chaim* Isaac Luria, the Sixteenth century Lion of Safed, wrote "Not the *Ayn Sof* (a word for Eternal) itself is dispersed in the nether worlds but only a radiance which emanates from Him." Gershom Scholem wrote:

> Between the World of Atziluth and that of Beriah and similarly between each of the following ones there is a curtain or partition wall ...the power which emanates from the substance passes through the filter of the curtain. This power then becomes the substance of the next world of which again only the power passes into the third and so through all four spheres. These garments of the divinity are no longer substantially one with God.

Between each world is a curtain, a permeable gate. The form taken for this gate in *The Hebrew Book of the Dead* is water, the great Sea of Ending that parts before the children of Israel, and the Sea of Descent, the Jordan, that parts for the renewed soul re-entering life in the Promised Land.

The World closest to the Throne of Glory is the World of Atziluth or Emanation.The three Worlds coming out of Atziluth take their names from the Book of Isaiah." I have created (*Beriah)* him for my glory, I have formed (*Yetzirah*), yea, I have made (*Assiyah*) him.

What does it mean to create, to form, to make? The prophet Isaiah says *He forms light and creates darkness.* In the process of forming light, God has brought into being, created, darkness. Rabbi Aryeh Kaplan, commenting on the *Bahir* says the concept of creation means "something from nothing," while formation is "something from something."

Of the World of Atziluth we may know nothing, It is shrouded in deep mystery, its radiance filtered through a curtain of thick darkness and chaos. It is like the ark of the Torah in our own World of Assiyah, guarded by flaming cherubim above, shielded by the curtain of separation. Like the Torah it is both before our eyes and utterly hidden. Within the ark is the Torah with its mantle and silver crowns and upon the scroll of the Torah, written in flaming letters on the skins of sacrificial animals, are the holy words, the *sod* and the *peshat*, the words that both hide and reveal the worlds of *The Hebrew Book of the Dead*. For the Torah itself is not the mantle or silver crowns or ink or skin. It is utterly before us and utterly hidden.

The World of Atziluth is both beyond us and *karov meod*, very near. In relation to the system of Worlds we stand as less than a simple protein in a single cell on a human finger. Though living, that protein cannot know the cell in which it lives. How then could it conceive of the skin, the knuckle itself, or the finger's articulating joints, the intricacies of the ligaments, nerves and muscles below, the electronic biochemical processes of that finger of which it is a negligible part?

And even if it could, even if this simple protein could make that impossible leap, it could never, structurally or functionally, conceive of the whole hand of which it is part, the fingering for a guitar chord, the fist clenched in anger, the delicate touch needed for surgical repair of a heart. It is only a simple protein, an amino acid building block.

How much less, then, could that single protein know the muscle, bone, nerve and tendon of an arm swinging a weapon, digging a post hole, embracing a child? How could it conceive of an entire body or the person within?

So much infinitely less are we literally, in this mass of universe. In this swarm of multitudes of Worlds we are far less than than a single sub-atomic particle within that simple protein.

We may be forever in dark ignorance of the higher Worlds and yet in each of us is all. We are joined to the whole, part of all Creation. Does not all the information necessary to create a complete human being rest coiled in the transcripted DNA codes within the nucleus of that single cell?

A reflected glimpse of the World of Creation — Beriah — that World in which the Divine spirit calls all into being, may be seen in the majestic opening of the biblical Book of Genesis. But of Yetzirah, the World flowing out of Beriah, that thundering airy fiery world surrounding our own world, that engulfing womb whose shadows and echoes color our own, we are on much more intimate terms. For the World of Yetzirah we feel great longing and trepidation, homesickness and hope for return. The World of Formation — Yetzirah — is the mediating World, the World of Angels, in which Creation is formed into its manifold parts. It is the setting for much of *The Hebrew Book of the Dead* and, for that matter, virtually all of the Hexateuch.

The fourth World, in a sense the culmination of the process of Creation, is the World of Assiyah, the natural World of Action, of Making and Doing, the world of space and time. The world we perceive in this life. We may not understand the ground on which we stand right here in the World of Assiyah, but we do know it is the ground and that we stand and that is enough for a beginning. In the World of Be-ing, we are.

Angels

There are frequent exchanges between the Worlds of Yetzirah and Assiyah in Hebrew Scripture, often through the medium of angels, generally called *malachim* or messengers. In *The Hebrew Book of the Dead* the chief angel is Moses, or Mosheh. (See Bazak Twenty-one, where Moses is sent as a messenger to the Children of Israel, or again in Bazak Twenty-seven: "I place my angel before you. My Name (*shmi*) is in him.") Moses mediates between God and the Children of Israel. Other angels are perceived ascending to Yetzirah in "Jacob's Ladder" (Bazak Nine), and others simply arise to direct Asaph to Dothan and slavery (Bazak Thirteen).

That there are angels and Worlds not available to our perception, our understanding, seems no more disputable than there are galaxies, electrons, and viruses. Angels frequently act to convey the influences of higher Worlds and reflect the influences of this world. At the time *The Hebrew Book of the Dead* was first told, the human heart had available to it a freshness of vision not yet subverted by the intellect. God and angels freely walked the Earth and all life was sacred.

The Bazakim

The Hebrew Book of the Dead is a reading of the Hebrew Scripture that takes selections from the sourcetext and presents each in direct translation. Bazak is a Hebrew word meaning "flash," as in a flash of lightning. It was used in the first edition of *The Hebrew Book of the Dead* to indicate the sudden flash of illumination that would illuminate a portion of the journey. The origin of this term is found in the opening of the biblical Book of Ezekiel.

The Hebrew Book of the Dead contains some 120 lines of Scripture distributed in 44 segments or *b'zakim* (b'-zah-KEEM). The complete text, of very great antiquity, is contained in the first six books of the Hebrew Bible.

The Hexateuch contains a clear and straightforward story line that extends from the creation of Heaven and Earth, preceding the formation of a living human, to the burial of Joseph's bones in Shechem. Between those two events stand the rise and fall of the first human, *ha-adam* — a creature made of *ruach* and *adamah*, the spirit of God and dust of the Earth — and the journey of purification and renewal taken by the soul on its way home.

Along with direct translation and citation for the biblical origins, each *bazak* is presented with the original Hebrew text. The twelve *bazakim* selected for translation and commentary in this edition of *The Hebrew Book of the Dead* are known as *In the Wilderness* for each *bazak* sheds light on our own path through the desert wilderness, the path that awaits us beyond the Sea of Ending.

The twelve *bazakim* open with five *bazakim* from the World of Beriah, the Creation bazakim, which are found

12

in the biblical Book of Genesis. The five following *ba-zakim*, like the very great bulk of the whole *Hebrew Book of the Dead*, are set in the World of Yetzirah. This is the landscape of the Book of Exodus. The two concluding *bazakim*, set in the World of Assiyah, can be found in the Book of Joshua.

The twelve *bazakim* raise and resolve the central issues of *The Hebrew Book of the Dead*: Where did we come from, what are we doing here, and where are we going? As with all the Torah from which they derive, they appear to be gifts of infinite value from the source of Being.

For continuity, short narratives link these *bazakim* together, supplying the biblical context for all forty-four *bazakim*. Following presentation of each *bazak* in this collection, there are commentaries and notes. Basic knowledge of Kabbalah is useful to follow some of the nuances of the text but constructs of Kabbalah are less necessary to an understanding of the message of the *bazakim* than an open mind and searching heart.

Finally, there are practical applications to *The Hebrew Book of the Dead*. Emerging from these *bazakim* is an expanded view of the Worlds, a view that includes access to the World of Yetzirah beyond the Gates of Death. Inherent in this view is the potential to enter upon a renewed relationship with God based on direct experience of a World from which we have come and to which we are headed all the days of our life. To that end, included in this edition is a section from the Book of Psalms, "Song of Ascents" and a meditative workshop, "How to Find God," applying kabbalist concepts of the Tree of Life.

The Hebrew Book of the Dead, safely hidden in the heart of Hebrew Scripture, has been before us from ancient times. A thousand years before the birth of Jesus, when David was king in Jerusalem, this book was more than a thousand years old. It is a record of the covenant of God's love.

Come, see.

The Tree of Life

A mong the most ancient myths of the Hebrews is the story of the Tree of Life, placed in the Garden of Eden. This Tree is intimately associated with the waters above and the waters below.

According to the Bahir, a Twelfth century text, "This Tree represents the Powers of the Blessed Holy One, one above the other. Just like a tree brings forth fruit through water, so the Blessed Holy One increases the Powers of the Tree through water. "

From the hidden World of Atzilut, the World of Emanation briefly described in the opening lines of the Torah, the powers and potencies of Creation are distributed in a supernal Tree whose counterpart is found in Eden. The Tree itself connects the Worlds, its roots stretching down to the Lower Worlds, its trunk extending through this World and its branches and foliage reaching up to the celestial Worlds.

The tree is a symbol of eternal life, its sap the juice of life. Throughout the ancient Middle East, groves of trees were considered sacred and worshipped.

The Tree of Life forms the axis of the *The Hebrew Book of the Dead.* Just as there is a Tree of Life, an *aytz-chai,* there is a Tree of Death. In Hebrew, the word for this tree is *aytzmot,* translated as "skeleton" or bones. Literally, the word is made up of *aytz* (tree) and *mot* (death).

When the biblical Joseph asks his kin to bring up his bones to the Promised Land, there to bury them in the field of his father, he is asking to have his Tree of Death planted that it may bring forth new life.

In the central story, this Tree of Death must be raised from the earth and carried across the desert wilderness, into the World of Yetzirah, the World of Formation, to be purified before it is planted in the Promised Land to burst into new life. (See Bazak Seventeen: A Tree of Death.)

There is another meaning to the biblical Tree, a meaning touched on by Eric Gutkind in *The Body of God.* The first human, ha-adam, ate of the Tree of Knowledge but did not touch the Tree of Life. From the one, ha-adam gained understanding of good and evil and all manner of technologies, but by-passed the Tree of Life itself. Had ha-adam eaten of the fruit of the Tree of Life this mud creature would live forever. Gutkind writes:

> In modern terms, it means that we wanted first to have knowledge, we wanted to know, we wanted to acquire something...and after security life will come...What comes after we have acquired security, after we have got something, after we have transformed every-thing into a thing, what follows is again al-ways a thing and not life. Life does not come.

Here near the beginning of *The Hebrew Book of the Dead,* in the story of the two trees in the middle of the Garden of Eden, the story's central theme is sounded. We confront our duality as creatures compounded of dust and holy spirit. We can choose life in the unfolding be-ing of Creation, or we can choose death and slavery.

Summary: Bazak One

בראשית ברא אלהים את השמים ואת הארץ
In the beginning God created the heavens and the Earth.

In this first instant of Creation, the universe blooms, unfurling from the single fixed unknowable Place that is God. And, just as we have learned from our science textbooks, the earth was unformed, a seething gaseous cauldron soon to cool and sustain life. This is the beginning of *The Hebrew Book of the Dead,* opening when the world is still dark, permitting us a vision over the Creator's shoulder as the great separations are made. *Let there be light.* And light appears and is separated from the darkness. It is the first day.

Let the Waters be separated and they are divided, separating the Worlds.

In these first lines, the outline of the Four Worlds emerges. The World of Emanation or Atziluth is the unknowable domain of the Lord of the Universe. It is from this World that light and the waters come.

This is the primal light and the primal waters, not the light that radiates from our Sun, not the waters that toss in the dark ocean beds. The pure light and waters of the World of Atziluth filter through all the Worlds.

The second World revealed in these first lines is the World of Creation or Beriah. In this World the potencies of Atziluth flow to the lower Worlds. The World of Beriah, seen here as the field in which God brings forth the works of Creation, is the mediating World between God and Creation.

The third World revealed in the opening lines is the World of Yetzirah, the World of Formation, the domain of angels, the world of our dreams and intuitions. The World of Yetzirah, brought into being by the division of the waters, encompasses our own World of Assiyah, the World of Action, of time and space, making and doing. In perceiving this division of Worlds, direct Hebrew translation of Scripture is most helpful. Commonly, Genesis 1:6 is read, "Let there be a firmament in the midst of the waters." The purpose of this firmament is to divide the upper Worlds from the lower Worlds. In Hebrew, the word for firmament is רקיע, *raki'a*. The *raki'a* separates the waters between Atziluth and Beriah on the one hand and Yetzirah and Assiyah on the other.

But what is a *raki'a*? Various uses of similar Hebrew forms convey the sense of something stamped, stretched out (Psalms 136:6) or an object that is beaten thin (Numbers 17:3). While a firmament, deriving from the Latin *firmamentum*, or supporting post, suggests a solid mass, the Hebrews looked at the *raki'a* differently

"...And over the heads of the living creatures there was the likeness of a *raki'a*, like the color of the terrible ice, stretched forth over their heads above," wrote the Prophet Ezekiel (1:22). Daniel (12:23) refers to the "brightness of the *raki'a*." A cold, bright, stretched out membrane is much like the sky might look to the Ancient Hebrews.

The division of the Waters — and thus, the Worlds — by the *raki'a* will soon find its analogue in the story of *The Hebrew Book of the Dead* where the Sea of Ending divides the World of Assiyah from the World of Formation, opening a path to the soul after death of the body.

Reflection: The Light of Creation
יהי אור *Y'hi Ohr -- Be Light*

The unfolding of this Light of Creation, emanating through all the Worlds, bears with it the present streaming moment. Creation is an explosive, continual process, leaving destruction in its wake.

The on-rushing Light of Creation endlessly mixes with the decaying products of its passage, for nothing is finally made or destroyed, and all things change. For us, living as the Light of Creation in decaying bodies of earth and water, it is as if we were at an intersection between Worlds, like tidepool creatures that exist only at the thin membrane of land and sea, neither water nor earth but sharing in each. The primal Light flowing through the World of Formation filters through that intersection and its effect on us in the World of Action is transformational.

For the Ancient Hebrews, the desert tabernacle, the Ark, and the sacrificial altar were consecrated as fixed entrances for the Light, holy places where the presence of the Lord of the universe could be felt. It was the spirit, the *ruach,* invested in those objects that made them holy. Their power did not extend to Nineveh and Rome when they were broken up and carried off. Where then are those holy intersections in our own clangorous times?

There are intersections of time, seasons to set aside our affairs and rejoice in the day the Lord has made. The Sabbath is such a time. The birth of a child is such a time.

And there are times of shock, separation, and calamity that open us to the Light. In all our days, we need only be aware to sense the Light flowing over us like a benediction.

And there remains the memory of holy places on Earth — temple ruins and walls, gravesites, buildings, battlefields, monoliths, reliquaries of the spirit. Covered over with war and blood, blackened with smoke, walls pocked with stones and cannon shell, these places of the Earth are coveted by our earthly longings long after the *ruach* that made them holy has departed. In our long history we have soaked the earth with the blood of those who would take our earth memories from us. And yet in the end, both the memories and the earth are gone. Where is the Ark today, the crown of thorns?

All flesh is grass. Only the Spirit, the ruach, of God is forever.

The effulgent Light is always with us, for the most holy intersection is within, the breath and beating heart continually announcing the Presence of God in our lives. Often, it takes a broken heart and contrite spirit to hear. It was not as a prince flush with power but as a fugitive shepherd alone in a strange land that Moses saw the Light break out into the world. The Light at the burning bush in the desert is part of the natural processes of the world where everything that lives, burns. The miracle of the burning bush is that the light of its burning is made visible. To choose life is to see the unfolding Light.

Living this life is to straddle two Worlds. The airy world of the Spirit blowing in the winds of the universe and the earthen world of the Flesh, pumping its fluids and grunting its wastes on to this composting planet, both reside in a single body of mud, a body of mineral, water, and earth.

But what of the fire, what of the air, the pneumatic whistling in our lungs, the burning in our belly and hearts, igniting the bubbling sweetbreads in our skull, what of hatred and what of love? They are all resident in this single mud body strung with electric neurons from stem to stern, filled with slimy slick tubes and tendrils that switch and feed a billion gnawing, breathing cells.

The Word is very near, in your mouth and in your heart that you may do it.

Our life is not in our body. The eye, that vitreous gelatinous orb, cannot see at all. A hundred million pupils, retinas, and corneal lenses can see no more than a rock or grain of sand blowing over the crest of a dune. Unplugged from the switchboard of the Lord, the eye cannot see nor the ear hear. The Light comes from another World and flows alike over the living and the void. The living Spirit briefly blows through myriad creatures and carries the Light on its breath.

We have known Light before our birth, in the dark formations of the womb, in the pressurized space cabin of the salty oceanic womb of our fetushood, plugged by a single connection into a distant host, accompanied by the lub-dub beat of an in-and-out heart. Squeezed in darkness into the long birth canal, we burst through salty waters in our long descent into the distant Light of this World of Time. Sliding down the ramp of birth, squished between the omphalos and fundament of our host mother, we emerge into the breaking Light, the rosy fingered dawn where forceps, milky breasts, pain, and awful beauty await us in the World of Action, the World of Assiyah.

In salt and blood and water are we made and born to feel the agony and great joy of the breath that fills our sticky lungs as we suck in the Spirit burning through all the worlds, the *ruach* of the Lord of Creation.

Such an anomaly are we. Showered in the blazing Light of Creation, we blunder our way through our days, creating and destroying, building and smashing our way blindly through a world in which darkness surrounds the nucleus of all our cells.

Bazak Two
בזק ב' מים
Mayim — *Waters*

ויאמר אלהים יקוו המים מתחת השמים אל־מקום
אחד ותראה היבשה ויהי־כן ויקרא אלהים ליבשה
ארץ ולמקוה המים קרא ימים

And God said, "Gather the waters under the heavens in one place and let the dry land be seen," and so it was. And God called the dry land Earth and the gathering of waters Seas.

— *Genesis 1:9, 10*

23

Commentary: Bazak Two
המים
Mayim - Waters

In Bazak One, taken from the opening lines of the Book of Genesis, we are granted a glimpse into the World of Beriah, the World of Creation. In Bazak Two we enter upon the bazakim (b'-zah-KEEM) of Formation, the World of Yetzirah.

It is here that materials already created become available to form the elements of the universe. The five realms created by God in Bazak One are Light, Darkness, Heaven, Earth and the Waters.

With separation of the Waters, the dry land emerges. Water and earth are the materials from which living beings will emerge.

In Bazak One, when darkness was upon the face of the Earth, the *ruach,* the Spirit of God, hovered over the face of the Waters. These are the Waters of Life. The separation of the Waters, the Waters above and the Waters below, create Heaven, a World beyond Earth.

Description of the *raki'a* in the middle of the waters, dividing the waters from the waters, is the Hebrew vision of a higher, encircling World. Rashi (Rabbi Solomon ben Isaac, an eleventh century, much loved French commentator on Hebrew Scripture) considers Genesis 1:6 to mean, "the middle of the waters is a division between the upper waters and the Earth-bound waters." It is a division between Worlds.

The opening of the dry land in *The Hebrew Book of the Dead* signals the beginning of new life, the blending of the waters with the earth. This land is called the *yabbashah*. At the start of the Exodus, when the Hebrews approach the Sea of Ending, Pharaoh's troops at their back, the land that is revealed by the parting of the seas is also called the *yabbashah*. It is the virgin earth that leads to a new World.

At the far end of the *midbar*, the desert wilderness, lies another body of water, the Jordan River, the Waters of Descent. Here, too, as the priests bearing the Ark prepare to cross the river, the waters separate, revealing the virgin earth, for once again a life is beginning in a new World.

In the *Sefer Yetzirah*, the ancient Book of Formation, Water is established as one the three great Mother letters of the Hebrew alphabet: Aleph (א), Mem (מ), and Shin (ש). "From them go forth Air (Shemayim, ש), Water (Mayim, מ) and Fire (Aysh, א). "

Once the virgin earth is opened, once the earth is revealed, it is compounded with Air, Water and Fire to produce sentient life.

It is in the division of the waters that life, derived from the descent of the Infinite Light of the *Ayn Sof*, the Eternal, drifting through the worlds, is formed. The Eternal, says Gershom Scholem, is "the absolute perfection in which there are no distinctions and no differentiations."

Y'hi Ohr, Let there be light. This first emanation, this first manifestation of the Eternal, brings into being the separations that create the tensions and possibilities of our life in the flesh. The division of the life waters, and the opening of the virgin earth set the stage for the creation of ha-adam, the human being made of mud and the spirit of God.

Bazak Three

בזק ג׳ נפש חיה

Nefesh Chayah - A Living Soul

ויברך אלהים את־יום השביעי ויקדש אתו
כי בו שבת מכל־מלאכתו אשר ברא אלהים
לעשות...ואד יעלה מן־הארץ והשקה את־כל־פני
האדמה וייצר יהוה אלהים את־האדם עפר מן־האדמה
ויפח באפיו נשמת חיים ויהי האדם לנפש חיה...
אלהים ברא אתו זכר ונקבה ברא אתם
ויקרא את־שמו אדם

And God blessed the seventh day and made it holy,
for in it He rested from all the labor of Creation in
which creating God made...And then there rose up
from the land a mist that watered the whole face of
the ground (ha-adamah). And the Lord YHVH
formed a mud creature (ha-adam) from the dust of
the ground (ha'adamah) and breathed into its nos-
trils the breath of life and the mud creature became
a living soul... The Lord created it, male and fe-
male created He them, and called their name Adam.

— *Genesis 2:3; 2:6,7; 1:27, 5:2*

Commentary: Bazak Three
לנפש חיה
Nefesh Chayah - A Living Soul

In Bazak Three *The Hebrew Book of the Dead* enters on the first and final mystery. Where have we come from when expelled bloody and gasping from the womb, and where are we bound when our spirit leaves our body? With all we may know of the codes transcribed in our genes, the ancestral traits engraved on our souls, to this day, of our origins and our destination, our beginnings and endings, we know less than the Ancient Hebrews knew four millennia ago.

This being could not be formed until the mist arose from the earth for God made this mud being from the water and dust and breathed the breath of life into its nostrils so it lived. In *Nefesh Chayah*, we glimpse the formation of the living soul.

This Being, created of earth and water infused with the *ruach haShem*, the Breath of God, feeling the Light of being and the pangs of many hungers, will soon lumber to its feet.

This is the Being who will kill and love, scheme and dream and go down to the pit in Goshen and be lifted up. This mud being will be carried off and placed in a dungeon in Egypt and rise to great power only to return to the dust to await passage into new life — this Being and no other. Look on it kindly, for it is us, created and formed to act in the world, and in our days can be seen the hand of the Creator of all Being

Now, near the beginning of *The Hebrew Book of the Dead*, this first naked soul, about to enter the earth and water of Being, is destined to be the container of the Word, the Beath of God in its mouth and rivers of blood beating in its heart, descending, to do the Word in this world, the World of Assiyah.

And when its work in the Kingdom of Assiyah is finished, the *Nefesh Chayah*, the living soul, will cross the Sea of Ending into the *Midbar*, the desert wilderness, and face many trials to purge its soul of slavery. For in the early days of passage across the wilderness, the soul still clings to the aromatic earth of the body, inhabited, loved, and fed. The soul mourns for its shell and beloved companion left behind in the World of Assiyah.

Beyond the Gates, the towering Sea of Ending, we return home and get clear of the clods of clay and dried grass of the fields still clinging to us, until, at home again, at home in the Body of God again, we find ourselves in the World of Yetzirah, the airy World of Formation. Most of us, like Asaph, the Dreamer King of *The Book of the Dead*, will reenter the World of Assiyah, to act. And for that we need bodies of earth and water, human bodies attached to the soul with ropes of pain.

The Light flowing from the Eternal plays upon the virgin earth exposed by the parting of the primal Seas and from the earth and water a Being is formed.

In all our passages, we depend on the Light permeating the World of Assiyah where our bodies of earth and water are suffused with the spirit and light of the Eternal so we may Be.

Y'hi Ohr! Be Light! The Word breaks out into Light, explodes in universes in nanoseconds. It is exploding still. The light falling gently through the cosmos, irradiating the planets with terrible brilliance, spirals through columns of galaxies rising through the empty heavens in colonnades of burning gas, roman candles in the Milky Way, echoes of distant Worlds unseen from any part of this universe, far falling Worlds bathed in the Light of the Eternal. Floating, spiraling down through the Worlds, this is the Light that calls us home. This Light, is it not God's love?

Before this Light there was the *Ayn Sof*, the Eternal One, alone without decay, without becoming, unknowable and there was Darkness over the face of the Void. The *Book of the Dead* tells us this is a place we cannot come to. This is the unknowable place of the first Bazak. The Hebrews simply called it the *Makom,* the Place.

Genesis, The Book of the Beginning, opens from God's perspective above the uncreated Heavens and ends with Asaph the beloved, the chosen bearer of the blessing, placed in a coffin in the Land of Bondage in the lowest dust of the earth.

It is the story of each life, proceeding from its uncreated state, to formation in the earth and water of our flesh, infused with the breath of the living God, inevitably to die and disassemble, reduce, return into constituent elements, body to body, spirit to spirit. This is the revealed Book.

This one death could be the death of any other Being no longer burning in the World of Assiyah. One can stand for all, for are we not all composed of the same earth and water, our hearts beating to a rhythm that comes from outside us, and does not one *ruach* infuse all our tissues?

The Prophet Isaiah says, "All flesh is grass."But what of all the jokes and sly looks, what of love and wild joys? Where have they gone?

"And all its loveliness is as the grass of the fields. The grass withers, the flower fades because the breath of the Lord blows on it. But the word of the Lord stands for ever."

What comfort is there in that? Even if we are, in our core living selves, the Word, what comfort in losing our loved ones, what hope is there for any of us, what rationale for the children stuffed into railroad cars, for tortured prisoners, for grieving parents?

And when this sojourn on Earth is over and we are finally out of this bright and noisy material world, this dark charade of blind desire and fear, do we suddenly get it, do we find it a great joke on the mangled children, the frightened mindless old, the sick and degenerate we leave behind?

Ecclesiastes says, "For that which befalls the son of man befalls beasts. Even one thing befalls them. As one dies so dies the other. Yes, they have all one *ruach*...all go to one place. All are of the dust and all return to dust."

So, does nothing happen in all our life together except the blowing of a wind and the scuttling of dead leaves at the end with none to hear and none to care?

The Radiance fell on the earth and water and breathed the *ruach* into this Being and made a person. And at the end of its few days on Earth, in this bottom, beautiful pit in the Kingdom of Assiyah, at the end of its few days when its body of earth and water falls away, this soul shall stand forth and appear at the gates of the Sea of Ending.

That is the Word of this ancient book. The angel of the Lord YHVH shall rise in exultation at our *aliyah*, our going up, to welcome us back from our brief descent to the Material world, to accompany us in our wanderings in the Midbar, home in the Body of God.

The Word is very near to you, in your mouth and in your heart that you may do it.

The formation of the soul begins with the breath of life, the *nishmat chayyim*. With this breath comes revelation, for we know this living breath is not of the earth and is not ours alone but it is a temporary gift of *ruach*, of wind-spirit, on which our days are strung.

The words of Bazak Three confirm what we have known all our days. Our Soul, our innermost being, is made of the breath of God.

The formation of the human soul described in this bazak — the compound nature of the breath spirit fused with an earth and water human body — sets in motion the vast epic that is *The Hebrew Book of the Dead*. An understanding of the Ancient Hebrew view of the soul and the inherent struggle resulting from its incarnation is intimately bound up in the kabbalistic system of Worlds.

The Anatomy of the Soul

Within traditional Kabbalah, the Soul has three parts —- the *ruach*, the *nefesh*, and the *neshamah*.

The root description is purely biblical. The *ruach HaShem* the Wind-Spirit of God, hovers over the face of the Waters. And then YHVH made a human of earth and water and blew into the nostrils the God-Soul (the *neshamah*). The God-Soul is carried on the *ruach*, the

35

Wind-Spirit, the fundamental energy field suffusing all being. The result of this process is the creation of a living soul, a *nefesh chayyah.* Within the *nefesh*, or individual life itself, is the spirit, the *ruach* that flows in and out, connecting its untouchable deepest God-Soul, the *neshamah*, with the shell of bodily existence. Within each life, within each *nefesh* is the totality of the soul.

It is this complex soul that thinks, creates, argues, loves. And it is the soul alone that voyages across Worlds, from our own World of Assiyah, the World of Time and Action, to the World of Yetzirah, the World of Formation, the world of souls. Beyond lies Beriah, the World of Creation, and beyond that stands the infinite mystery, the World of Atzilut, the unknowable source of Light and Being.

The soul's own essence is on an immense journey of becoming, influenced by and influencing all the Worlds in its passage.

> The first room in the Kingdom of ASSIYAH --
> its halls are made of Earth.
> The first room in the Kingdom of YETZIRAH --
> its halls are made of Air.
> The first room in the Kingdom of BERIAH --
> its halls are made of Water
> The first room in the Kingdom of ATZILUT --
> its halls are made of Fire.
>
> —Rabbi Nachman haTiktinner (HaRanit)

Y'hi Ohr. Be Light, and from the emanation of that light comes forth the Worlds. It is as if a liquid were poured through a vessel with many sections and all sections contain the liquid but some sections are closer to the source.

It is as if, says Aryeh Kaplan, "A breath leaves the glass-blower's lips, travels through his blowing tube as a wind, and finally rests in the object that he is forming, shaping it as he desires. The breath is the Neshamah-Breath...This is transmitted down to man in the form of a "wind" which is the level of Ruach-Windspirit. When it rests in man, it is called Nefesh-Soul, which comes from the root *nafash* meaning 'to rest'."

The neshamah is the Fire-Spirit, the Pure Soul, untouched in our life by our actions, returned at our disincarnation in its pure state, for it is in but not of this World.

Moses, the Angel Mosheh of the *Book of the Dead,* is a stranger in Assiyah for he is not of this World. In Midian with his father-in-law Jethro, he can say *ger hayiti b'eretz nochriYAH,* a wanderer am I in a Land estranged from God.

Bazak Three Bridges Three Worlds

With the creation of ha-adam in God's own image, the labor of Creation, the work of the World of Beriah, has been completed. At the opening of Bazak Three "God blessed the seventh day and made it holy for in it God rested from all the labor of Creation."

The ideal creation of a human being in the World of Beriah here begins to take physical shape in the World of Yetzirah.

"And the Lord YHVH וייצר, *vayitzer,* formed a mud creature (ha-adam) from the dust of the ground and breathed into its nostrils the breath of life and ha-adam became a living soul."

When the mud creature becomes a living soul it can act in the World of Assiyah, choose fruit from the Tree of Knowledge, lie, kill, love, and suffer.

There are many scenes in *The Hebrew Book of the Dead* drawn from this World of Assiyah. But the main landscape of this ancient epic is the World of Yetzirah. From earth to fire, across the parted waters, the *Hebrew Book of the Dead* takes us into *malkhut yetzirah,* the Kingdom of Souls, the World of Formation.

In this Kingdom we are newborn, strangers in a foreign land. We have come to this Midbar, this desert wilderness, to be transformed, to burn in the burning of the Lord. We wander and struggle in the World of Yetzirah until our delusions are burned away and we are ready to re-enter, across the waters, the World of Assiyah. There we will have a human body for there we have come to act.

At the end of our life, in leaving that body on the shores of Assiyah and crossing the Sea of Ending into the desert wilderness, we begin, again, the work of Yetzirah.

Leaving Egypt

In the Exodus of the children of Israel described in *The Hebrew Book of the Dead* disincarnation, the order and means of the Soul's separation from the body can be found.

Before the Soul can escape, the lintel of the doorway of each Israelite's house, and the two doorposts, the *mezzuoth,* must be struck with a hyssop branch dipped in blood, blood of the sacrificial lamb.

For it is in blood and through pillars of Water across the virgin earth, the *yabbashah*, that this birthing into Yetzirah shall take place, that the Soul shall change its abode. And just as the breath of expiration carries off our life on Earth, the *ruach* departs first.

In the biblical Exodus, it is the east wind that rises to separate the Waters permitting the children of Israel to pass over the dry earth.

Rabbi Nachman Tiktinner, HaRanit, says:

> We do not see the wind but the effects of the wind
> We do not see the fire but the residue of its burning
> Wind and fire are but the marks of passage
> We do not see the Soul but her marks of passage, shadows and echoes of her passage.

The Order of Separation

The order of separation of the Soul from the body reverses the order of formation. The *ruach,* the Wind-Spirit, which suffuses all the Worlds and on which all living things depend, departs on the expiring breath of the dying, carrying in its wake the *neshamah*, returning to her source.

The *nefesh* lingers, for she is tied to the body, identified with the body she has inhabited in all its days in Assiyah. In *The Hebrew Book of the Dead* the taste for meat, the desires for flesh, the longing for the leeks and cucumbers of Egypt are slavish delusions that prevail until the *nefesh* can separate from the body.

"At dusk you shall eat flesh and in the morning you shall be filled with bread and you shall know that I am YHVH, your God. "

In the World of Yetzirah, bread does not feed the body. There, food is manna, the incorporeal Angel Bread that drops from Heaven and does not grow from the Earth. Contemplating the difference between material bread and manna, between satisfying physical and spiritual hunger, we can come to understand the trials faced by the soul in the wilderness, separating from its bodily existence.

The order of separation in disincarnation also helps us to understand the anatomy of the soul in its reincarnation. For as we are unmade, so are we made. And in understanding this process we come to see sin as disease to which our Soul is subject.

For what is sin except that which stands between our Soul and God? We sin by turning away from God, by pride and greed and fear do we sin. *The Word is very near, in our mouth and in our heart that we may do it.* We sin by denying the Word that burns within us.

The prophet Isaiah said: *Your iniquities have separated you from God.*

Sin and the Pathology of the Soul

Diagnosis of disease of the Soul is made difficult by our inability to weigh and measure her dimension, for mass and volume are characteristic of the World of Assiyah.

But we are compensated by a far deeper and more immediate power — our ability to feel our own emptiness and despair when separated from God, our own elation when we leave the darkness and draw near.

The Single Commandment

The root cause of Soul disease has been related to the commandments of YHVH. Traditionally, there are 613 commandments in the Torah of the Hebrews. There were Ten Commandments received on Sinai. The prophet Micah reduced the basic commandments to three:

> He has shown you, O Man, what is good and what does YHVH require of you but to do justly and to love mercy and to walk humbly with your God.

And in his farewell address to the children of Israel, the Angel Mosheh reduced the commandments to essentially one: *devekuth*. Love YHVH and cleave *(devekah)* to Him (see Bazak Forty-one). Violation of this one commandment, and all the commandments that flow from it, sickens the Soul.

The major symptoms of Soul disease are despair, anxiety, headache, fatigue, depression. The body absorbs and reflects the struggles of the Soul in all three classes of disease:

Disease of Constriction, characterized by cruelty and the absence of pity or love. This disease is caused by inability to love the core God self through willfulness or disposition. Adin Steinsalz talks of the narrow passage of the throat:

> Thus a person can reach a very high level of truly understanding the greatness and goodness of God, but it can remain theoretical.

> The understanding may not be able to get
> through the narrow passage in order to affect
> the rest of the person, and this block will be a
> constant threat to health and well-being."

Disease of Excess or expansion, characterized by pride,
lust, and anger. Typically, diseases of the Soul stemming
from excess come from neglect of the God self in the high
blood of youth and passion, an imbalance in which the
earth body predominates.

Disease of Darkness or imbalance, characterized by deep
depression, the "dark night of the Soul." This is the most
painful disease of the Soul, a profound darkness brought
on by exile from God and identification with the earth
body and illusions of the physical world. "I will hide My
face from them," said the Lord.

What Are We that We May Sin?

Is not our soul knitted together, fused at the instant of
our conception? Our body, the receptacle and garment of
the soul, is determined significantly before birth, our size
and capacities to some extent determined by the DNA
transcription of messages at the molecular biological level,
by mandated pairings of protein, strands of polypeptides
in which may be read, as in cosmic tea leaves, the unroll-
ing of our days on Earth.

We are body and soul, and the mud body receives the
Nefesh for which it was destined just as the Nefesh enters
and actively forms the body.

> The purpose of the soul entering this body
> is to display her powers and actions in this
> world for she needs an instrument...Before

descending to this world the soul is ema-
nated from the mystery of the highest
level. While in this world she is completed
and fulfilled by this lower world. Departing this world, she is filled in the fullness
of all the worlds, the world above and the
world below.

At first, before descending to this world,
the soul is imperfect, she is lacking something. By descending to this world she is
perfect in every dimension.

> From *The Zohar,* Daniel Matt's translation, in
> *The Essential Kabbalah*

Ze'ev ben Shimon HaLevi says:

The cycle of life and death operates in sequence and so most souls are repeatedly returned to live on Earth in order to gain experience that cannot be had at the level of
pure Yetzirah. The...creative tension between
the angelic body of the psyche and the physical situation found on Earth can make possible things impossible in the non-material
Worlds above.

There is a deep reality to incarnation, to living on
Earth. It is the physical, immediate reality of our own
lives. When Abraham argues with God to save Sodom, he
says, "Behold, I have taken it upon me to speak to the
Lord and I am ashes and dust. " He is only expressing the
reality grasped by the Ancient Hebrews and brought
home to us today in each breath and heartbeat. The living
force within us is not made of dust and ashes nor earth
and water but of God. For when we depart our body, the

earth-water garment remains as it was, dressed as it was, weighing what it did while we still winked and gasped, joked and ate. And yet we are entirely gone.

When the Spirit departs, the body closes down to its cellular depths, extinguishing consciousness and function until all that remains is the oxidation of the cells and the orbiting of subatomic particles, flashing stars in the subatomic night.

Consciousness leaves. Then function. The *neshamah* is gone, drawn by the *ruach*, departed on the last breath, and only briefly does the *nefesh* linger. For we truly are a piece of God placed in the universe, set as a candle, a burnt offering. For everything that lives, burns. The beauty of that burning reflects the light of Creation.

We burn in pain and joy in all our days in the Body of God.

We are fused from two Souls, set on our karmic course by knitting together the genetic history of our ancestors in our flesh and in our bones and in our Nefesh. In this state we plop wet and bloody and blind into the World of Assiyah to do the work of YHVH.

Again, from the *Sefer Yetzirah*:

> Three Mothers: Aleph (א), Mem (מ), Shin
> (ש) are in the universe: air, water and fire.
> He caused the letter Aleph to reign over Air
> (*ruach*).
> He caused the letter Mem to reign over
> Water (*mayim*).
> He caused the letter Shin to reign over Fire
> (*aysh*).

Body and Soul in New York City

The ghosts of memory are lingering angels. When I think of the Upper West Side in New York, or the Café Figaro in Greenwich Village or Pete's Tavern in Gramercy Park, I feel the coordinates of a time of grace, because I was very young when I lived there and those places light up my heart to this day. Those were high-blooded and slightly dangerous days on the proscenium of New York, with exits and entrances in yellow cabs that would stream under the PanAm building on Park Avenue to stop at dark expensive restaurants. I can still feel winter walks, when hand in hand with a warm lover, I heard frozen feet in leather shoes crunching the new snow on Central Park West.

New York then was a world of ardent hopes, high hearts in rags and wild hair, the smell of corner hot dogs steaming from a cart mixing with the steam from manhole covers in the street, the incense censer of Manhattan. That world no longer truly exists. It has been swept away to make room for a new world of different languages and scripts, a world for other actors to strut upon its bedrock for a time. And those of us gone are mostly forgotten, quickly out of mind and irrelevant. But my ancient New York lives this very night in California, and in living whispers to me of the human soul.

The coordinates of our past lives can be plotted against the chart of our passage through this world. My body, the body that played upon that New York stage, has long gone, along with the streets and the taverns and the fumes of salty hot dogs simmering in greasy water. Gone and yet

45

so easy to recall. For the *nefesh* is bound up and knit together with our body in an intimate embrace. It is the part that says "Me" when we think of ourselves and the part that thinks when we think and Sees and observes.

It is all those parts and it is who we are on Earth.

After the *Nefesh* Is Gone

And when we are no longer on Earth, when even the lingering *nefesh* departs, what of the body? After death, the body remains behind, in place, just as its toothbrush continues to jut out of the holder in its bathroom, just as its laundry and unpaid bills survive its passing. Shortly after death the body looks much the same and yet unplugged, discarded.

In all its abandoned vulnerability, its inertness, the body is not so small a thing. This holy habitation of the Soul, beloved and cleaned while we lived, stroked, dressed, paraded, was the instrument of our power in the world, required for love, sex, art, battle, nurturance, worship. It is no small thing to leave this body behind, an object left on a foreign shore. Those things we think most as being us — our face, our hands, our body — are beloved molecules, star-stuff and quarks lightly and loosely assembled.

The body grows inert. Separated from the Soul, soon to be nothing but earth and water.

Bereft of our Wind-Soul and our Fire-Soul we linger, a naked *nefesh* without even the water-earth garment of our sojourning on Earth. In common, we die and leave behind our dreams and cars, our jokes and toys and take with us a terrible longing.

The story we are told in the Holy Scripture of the Hebrews tells of the pain endured by the *nefesh* and its great joy in becoming whole, becoming human across the Waters of Descent.

Take the BMT to Brooklyn

New York, in its unfolding state, in the surrounding sensory presence of my youth, is gone. But here I sit on a Pacific shore, decades past, and can still hear the sound of subway wheels braking to a stop, see the color of gum trees turning copper in the Brooklyn autumn, breathe the smell of a new pink ball, licorice gum, my father's coat fresh from the cold.

Nothing is lost — not a life, not a city, not a breath, not a dream. Every blade of grass has a guardian angel, every neutrino a mission.

Summary: Bazak Four to Bazak Eight

I n these *bazakim* are the tales of early human life on Earth from Adam and Eve to Noah and the Flood. The Worlds had not yet fully separated and in those days the gods came down to breed with the daughters of men.

Abraham is introduced in Bazak Five. God promises that his descendents will be numerous as the stars but they will serve four hundred years in servitude before they can claim the Promised Land. This covenant is sealed in the flesh through circumcision. God tells Abraham His Name is El Shaddai.

Abraham proves his faithfulness in Bazak Six by his willingness to sacrifice his son Isaac.

In Bazak Seven, Esau and Jacob, twin contending sons, are born to Rebekah and Isaac.

Bazak Eight tells how the blessing — passed to Isaac by Abraham — was stolen by Jacob with the help of his mother. To avoid the wrath of his twin brother, Jacob flees. Before he leaves Canaan he has his first Divine visitation.

Bazak Nine
בזק ט׳   והנה סלם
Hinei Sulam   Behold, a Ladder

ויחלם והנה סלם מצב ארצה וראשו מגיע
השמימה והנה מלאכי אלהים עלים וירדים
בו והנה יהוה נצב עליו ויאמר אני יהוה אלהי
אברהם אביך ואלהי יצחק הארץ אשר אתה
שכב עליה לך אתננה ולזרעך והיה זרעך כעפר
הארץ ופרצת ימה וקדמה וצפנה ונגבה ונברכו
בך כל־משפחת האדמה ובזרעך והנה אנכי
עמך ושמרתיך בכל אשר־תלך והשבתיך
אל־האדמה הזאת

*And he dreamed, and behold, a ladder set up on the
Earth and the head of it reached to the Heavens.
And behold, angels of God rose up and descended on
it. And behold, the LORD stood beside him and
said, " I am YHVH, God of Abraham your father
and God of Isaac. The land on which you lie I shall
give to you and to your children. And your seed shall
be as the dust of the earth and you shall be spread as
the dust of the west and east, north and south and*

blessed shall be all families of the Earth in your children. And behold I am with you and will guard you in all that shall befall you and I shall bring you back to this land."

— *Genesis 28:12-15*

Commentary: Bazak Nine
והנה סלם
Hinei Sulam - Behold, a Ladder

The image of the Ladder, foot resting on the Earth, head reaching into Heaven, is that not the nature of our life? The parade of Angels rising and descending are a communal display of neighboring Worlds, accessible to one another, related. Soon *The Hebrew Book of the Dead* will shift its focus from these overarching Worlds and take us to the life of Asaph, son of Jacob, a dreamer who rises from the pit to great power.

Soon we will drift through the celestial curtains between the Worlds, and enter Yetzirah, the World of Formation, but for now there are only intimations, footfalls down the hall and angels gliding up and down a dream ladder.

Bazak Nine is prophetic as well as descriptive. What happens when you breathe the *ruach* of God into a being of dust and water? From Adamah, the golem, we see Adam the human being arise dazzled in the Light and stumble off into a life of murder, envy, lies, hope, and dreams.

Here, in Bazak Nine, the options available to this human being are further developed, the idea of going up (*aliyah*) and descending (*yeridah*) is expanded. "Behold, Angel *olim v'yordim*, going up and coming down." In *The Hebrew Book of the Dead* to go up means to rise, spiritually, to a higher world, as "Let us go up to Zion." To descend is to acquire a more earthly aspect, as in "Descend to Sheol" or "Go down to Egypt" or simply to step down, across the Waters of Descent, to become human in the Promised Land.

This is one of many dreams in the Hebrew Scripture. Just as we move in and out of the unconscious ocean of our dreams, as if from one world to another, so too did the Ancient Hebrews. But they recognized the power of this experience as a reflection of sacred intent, a means to enter direct communication with God. We are currently recovering from the purely psychological interpretation of dreams that prevailed in the nineteenth century, but once for us, too, dreams had the power to change the world.

Dreams are central in the history of the Covenant and the life of Jacob's chosen son, Asaph. ("Behold, the dreamer comes.")

In Bazak Nine, Jacob is assured that the blessing he stole from his brother, with the connivance of his mother, by deceiving his blind and dying father, has been truly deeded to him. He is told, as was his grandfather Abraham when first receiving the Covenant, "All the nations of the Earth shall bless themselves by your descendants."

Emphasizing the transfer of the Covenant from Abraham to Jacob, God says I am the Lord, the God of your father Abraham and the God of Isaac." The direct line from Abraham to Jacob is drawn. In a Book that rarely repeats itself, we are told that Jacob — liar, schemer, and fugitive though he may be — is truly the bearer of the Covenant. Surely the Hebrew peasant would want to know why, and yet nothing is said. There is no attempt to rationalize God's ways.

The final seal of approval is given to Jacob. God stands beside him and says, "I am with you, I will protect you." This is the universal covenant, the covenant spread over our days, ratified in each breath and heartbeat. Not that we will be kept in life, in Assiyah, but that God is with us and will protect us in all our journeys.

The prophetic elements in this dream are many. Where Abraham's descendants were to be as numerous as the stars and sand, Jacob's shall be "as the dust of the earth." Sforno (Obadiah Ben Jacob Sforno), the fifteenth century Italian master of the *peshat*, or literal and direct interpretation of Scripture, understands this to mean "only after your seed has reached the lowest depths of misery...and is treated like the dust of the earth will salvation come to them." The children of Jacob, called Israel, may not have become as numerous as the dust of the earth, but they have been ubiquitous.

What may be more prophetic is the clear announcement of a future *galut*, an exile. Announcement of this diaspora is made in *The Hebrew Book of the Dead* millennia before the Hebrews had entered their own land. And that announcement is made with chilling precision. " You shall spread to the west, east, north and south," and indeed the children of Israel would disperse in each of those directions until there was no place on Earth that did not have descendants of Jacob within its borders.

The impact of this massive diaspora and intermingling among the nations of the world is to spread the Name of God and teachings of Torah throughout all the Nations, spread not through preaching but through ties of blood. And those are the very words of this Bazak: "And blessed in your seed shall be all families of the earth." The Hebrew word *zarah*, or seed, is plain enough but the Rashbam (Rabbi Shmuel ben Meir, the twelfth century sage who was the grandson of Rashi) renders the term by one of its lesser used meanings, translating the the word as "graft," or "join." Literally the words read,"Then shall bless themselves, all families of the earth, in your joining."

And indeed that has been the case. The Mongols and Babylonians, Russians and Germans, Ethiopians and Persians, Turks and Goths have blessed themselves in the seed of Jacob and are blessing themselves still.

"Behold I am with you — *Hinani, Anochi imach* — and will bring you back to this land, for I will not leave you until I have done that which I have said to you I will do."

And so it was. Crushed and enslaved by the empires of Assyria, Babylonia and Rome, the children of Israel entered upon 2,000 years of exile until, as prophesied by the Prophet Isaiah, returned to the land in our own days, fulfilling Jacob's dream.

And when they came back to the Land of Israel did they not look like Turks, Armenians, Russians and Ethiopians, Persians and Huns, Mongols and Englishmen? For as the family of nations blessed itself with the seed of Israel, Israel would bless itself with the seed of the family of nations before the great Exile was brought to an end and the word of YHVH was fulfilled.

It could be argued that this text refers simply to the return of Jacob to Canaan. But the word of the Lord that must be fulfilled before YHVH has completed "all that which I have said to you I would do" includes the acquisition of the land, the diaspora and the return to the land. The land will not be acquired until after the time of Joshua, many centuries distant from the setting of this dream of a ladder reaching to the heavens.

The spreading across the four corners of the Earth won't occur until a thousand years after Solomon has completed the building of the Temple in Jerusalem and certainly not until Sargon carries off the Ten Tribes to Nineveh, not until Nebuchadnezzar destroys the Temple, not until Titus and his four Roman Legions break down the walls of Jerusalem.

It is only in our own days that the prophesied return to the land was completed. Never before in history did a people flow from all corners of the Earth to come back to the land they once occupied. But it was written and it came to pass. As in a dream, the Exiles came streaming back to the Land of Israel.

That return, following on two millenia of exile, on wanderings, pogroms and the Holocaust, seemed nothing less than a miracle, the fulfillment of an ancient prophecy embedded in the dream of a ladder.

בשוב יהוה את־שיבת ציון היינו כחלמים

B'shuv YHVH et-shivat tzyion haonu k'cholmim
When YHVH brought the Exiles back to Zion
we were as in a dream

Summary: Bazak Ten to Bazak Twelve

After his dream of the ladder, Jacob leaves Beer-Sheva in Canaan for Haran in the land of the Arameans and the house of his uncle Laban. There he falls in love with Rachel and marries her and her sister Leah. He prospers and some years later returns to Canaan with his wives, two maidservants, children, and many servants and cattle. With him is his favorite son, Joseph, referred to throughout *The Hebrew Book of the Dead* as Asaph, the Carried Off.

In Bazak Eleven, on the eve of crossing the waters of Jabbok into Canaan to face his brother Esau, Jacob wrestles with an angel and is renamed *Israel*, Struggler-with-God. He arrives in the city of Shechem and purchases the land where he sets up his tent and raises an altar to El, God of Israel. Rachel dies in childbirth, bearing a final son, Benjamin, to Jacob. Isaac dies and is buried by Esau and Jacob, now called Israel. Israel settles near Kiryat Arba in the Valley of Hebron in Canaan where Isaac had settled.

Israel loved Joseph best of all his sons and Joseph was hated by his brothers. Joseph had dreams in which he reigned over his brothers and all his family.

At the opening of Bazak Thirteen, Joseph has been sent to bring Jacob reports on the flock and his brothers. A man comes upon Joseph wandering in the fields and directs him to Dothan.

Bazak Thirteen
בזק י"ג הבור

Ha'Bor - The Pit

וימצאהו איש והנה תעה בשדה
וישאלהו האיש לאמר מה־תבקש ויאמר את־אחי
אנכי מבקש הגידה־נא לי איפה הם רעים ויאמר
האיש נסעו מזה כי שמעתי אמרים נלכה דתינה
וילך יוסף אחר אחיו וימצאם בדתן ויראו אתו מרחק
ובטרם יקרב אליהם ויתנכלו אתו להמיתו ויאמרו
איש אל־אחיו הנה בעל החלמות הלזה בא ועתה
לכו ונהרגהו ונשלכהו באחד הברות ואמרנו חיה רעה
אכלתהו ונראה מה־יהיו חלמתיו

A man found him and behold, he was lost in the field. Then the man asked him, saying, "What are you looking for? "And he said, "I am looking for my brothers. Tell me, please, where is the flock?" And the man answered, "They left from here for I heard them say, "Let us go to Dothan." And Asaph went after his brothers and found them in Dothan. And they saw him at a distance and before he came near they plotted against him to kill him. And they said, one brother to another, "Behold, this dreamer comes. Let us go now and kill him and throw him into one of the pits, and we will say an evil beast ate him and we shall see what will be his dreams."
— Genesis 37:15-20

Commentary: Bazak Thirteen

בזק י"ג הבור

Ha'Bor - The Pit

This *bazak*, with its backdrop of treachery and despair, expands our understanding of the critical role angels play in our earthly affairs. Asaph's brothers were jealous of him because he was the beloved son of their father's most beloved wife, and they hated him because of his dreams of power. But while they plotted his death and placed him in a desert pit with no water, they were also the instrument of his rise to power and their own transformation.

It took the intercession of an angel to bring it about. For Asaph was lost and the angel found him and directed him to his destiny.

In all the hierarchy of angels, from Metatron and the Archangels down to the lowest angel in the Cohort of the Lord, the sweetest is that angel assigned a single task, brought into being by the Word to perform a single act.

The Hebrew Book of the Dead is filled with angels, angels of fire and angels of cloud, angels that test and angels that lead. "I have placed my angel before you. Obey him for My Name is in him," is how our fate was assigned to Mosheh, the Angel of Rescue, called Moses.

The angels that lubricate the world's wheels are the *malachim* the messenger angels. When Jacob sends Asaph, the Carried Off, called Joseph, to Shechem to see his brothers he sets in motion the machinery of the Exodus. Shechem marks the beginning and end of *The Hebrew Book of the Dead.*

When Abraham comes to the Promised Land from

Haran, he arrives first in Shechem. Asaph goes toward Shechem to meet his fate, and an open field in Shechem is the place in which his bones shall be buried after the trials of the Midbar.

And a man found him and behold he was straying in the field and the man asked him, saying, What are you looking for? And he said, I seek my brothers. Tell me, please, where they feed their flocks. And the man said, They have journeyed from here for I heard them say, Let us go to Dothan.

Nachmanides (Rabbi Moshe ben Nachman) said the man was was an angel. By directing Asaph to his brothers he took the step necessary to fulfill God's plan. Relying on a text from the Book of Daniel, Rashi says the man is the Angel Gabriel. But identification may not be as important as realization, as knowing we are in the presence of an Angel of the Lord, an angel whose essence is hidden.

We are surrounded in our days by myriads of angels. "Mighty men and a host of angels are mustered with us," says the Dead Sea Scroll *The War of the Sons of Light.* Among the angels are beings formed from the incarnation of our thoughts and actions, the coalescence of Spirit into Time.

The creation of an angel in our world writes Adin Steinsalz in *The Thirteen Petalled Rose*:

> and the immediate relegation of this angel to another world is, in itself, not at all a super-natural phenomenon; it is part of a familiar realm of experience, an integral piece of life which may even seem ordinary and com-monplace because of its traditional rooted-ness in the system of *mitzvot* (command-ments) or the order of sanctity.
>
> When we are in the act of creating the an-gel, we have no perception of the angel being created and this act seems to be a part of the whole structure of the practical material

world in which we live. Similarly, the angel
who is sent to us from another world does
not always have a significance or impact beyond the normal laws of physical nature.

The Way of the Worlds

Determining the hierarchy of angels can be an arid and
disputatious exercise, one in which we can easily lose the
electric perception of God's Presence revealed through
His messenger. We can become sensitized to the intervening event that sets a scene in motion, a chance encounter
that changes our life, a fleeting peripheral vision of a messenger in motion.

There is a general way through which we can order our
understanding and come closer to the perception of angels in our life. We can be mindful of the Way of the
Worlds, a system that appears peculiarly kabblistic but in
fact resonates in each of us in our own terms. (That E, after all, does equal mc^2 should assure the most pragmatic
among us of the existence of Worlds beyond our perception.) Awareness of the Worlds of which we are an infinitesimal part can sensitize us to influences and beings in
our midst. The Worlds are one means of exploring the
spiritual nature of angels.

The World of Yetzirah, the setting for the desert wanderings, is, in Gershom Scholem's words, "the chief domain of the angels." Our own flesh and blood world, the
World of Assiyah, is furthest from the Upper Worlds, is
most hidden from the Throne of Glory. Here, our veiled
and thickened perceptions diminish our sensibilities, re-
ducing our awareness of the angels among us.

In the opening lines of Steinsalz' *Thirteen Petalled Rose*,
we read :

The physical world in which we live, the ob-
jectively observed universe around us, is only
a part of an inconceivably vast system of
worlds. Most of these worlds are spiritual in
their essence; they are of a different order
from our known world.

Crossing the impermeable boundaries of these worlds
are hosts of angels.

*And he dreamed and behold a ladder set up
on the earth, and the top of it reached to
heaven; and behold angels of God (Malachi
Elohim) going up and down on it.*

A man found him. Colorless, mysterious, a man arises
to find the lost boy and point the direction of Asaph's
destiny and then disappears, nameless forever.

Nor are angels ethereal beings. In my own life, I have
found this to be true. "We are angels to each other," said
Karen, my own Guardian Angel. "We are all angels to
each other one way or another," she said.

Summary: Bazak Fourteen - Bazak Sixteen

Joseph is raised from the pit and sold to a passing band of Ishmaelites. He is taken as a slave to Egypt where he serves Potiphar, an overseer in the house of Pharaoh. After a time Joseph is placed in charge of the household. His youth and beauty attract Potiphar's wife who, when rejected, falsely accuses Joseph of attempted rape.

Joseph is placed in prison. After some time, Pharoah's cupbearer and baker are put into prison and each has a prophetic dream correctly interpreted by Joseph. Later, when the Pharaoh has a troubling dream which his magicians are unable to interpret, his chief cupbearer, released from prison as Joseph prophesied, tells the Pharaoh of Joseph's powers.

Joseph is brought to the court, interprets Pharaoh's dreams as God's warning of a pending famine, and is immediately raised up by Pharaoh and placed in charge of all the land of Egypt. As Chief Vizier to Pharaoh, Joseph receives his brothers in the court as they seek relief from the famine.

In Bazak Fifteen Joseph is reconciled with them and brings all his brothers and their children and Jacob, called Israel, to live with him in Egypt. Before Jacob dies he asks Joseph to promise to take him up from Egypt to bury him in Canaan. After his death, Joseph has him embalmed and taken to Canaan and buried in Abraham's cave in the field of Machpelah.

Bazak Seventeen — containing the concluding lines of the biblical Book of Genesis — opens with Joseph calling his kindsmen together. He is anticipating his own death.

Bazak Seventeen
בזק ט"ז עצמת
A'tzmot - A Tree of Death

ויאמר יוסף אל־אחיו אנכי מת ואלהים פקד
יפקד אתכם והעלה אתכם מן הארץ הזאת
אל־הארץ אשר נשבע לאברהם ליצחק וליעקב
וישבע יוסף את־בני ישראל לאמר פקד יפקד
אלהים אתכם והעלתם את־עצמתי מזה וימת
יוסף בן־מאה ועשר שנים ויחנטו אתו ויישם
בארון במצרים

*And Asaph said to his kinsmen, "I die but God will
certainly remember you and bring you up out of this
Land to the land he promised to Abraham, Isaac,
and Jacob." And then Asaph caused the children of
Israel to take an oath, saying, "God will surely visit
you and so you shall raise up my bones from here."
And Asaph died one hundred and ten years old.
And they embalmed him and placed him in a coffin
in Egypt.*

— *Genesis 50:24-26*

Commentary: Bazak Seventeen
בזק י"ז עצמת
Atzmot - A Tree of Death

Genesis, the Book of the Beginning, opens far above the chaos and desolation over the face of the deep and moves to the Creation of light and all the Worlds. The book moves from inconceivable heights to end in a coffin in the Lower Kingdom.

Asaph has risen from the pit in the desert and again from Pharaoh's dungeon to great power. Here he is once again certain of being raised up but he needs to be brought back to the land of the Covenant. The return of Jacob's bones to Canaan fulfils the promise YHVH made to return him to the Promised Land. But now the Covenant rests with Asaph and to protect it means bringing him through Yetzirah, across the Midbar to Canaan.

He tells his brethren they will make *aliyah,* that God will "bring them up" out of the land once their time of servitude is over. Before dying, he exacts a promise from his kinsmen to raise up his bones and bring them across with them.

So Joseph died, being a hundred and ten years old and they embalmed him and he was put in a coffin in Egypt. The Hebrew word is not "coffin" but the far different word *Ah'ron,* an Ark. Joseph, known as Asaph the Carried Off, was placed in an Ark for his bones will voyage across the wilderness to the Promised Land.

The Hebrew word for bones, עצמת *atzmot,* is used figuratively, as in "bone of my bone and flesh of my flesh." *Atzmot* is also used literally to mean skeleton. The word is made of two parts, עץ *aytz* and מת *mot,* the words for "tree" and "death." To consider the human skeleton with its roots and branches, head and limbs and trunk a Tree of Death is not at all an obscure concept. What is conveyed by this image of the Tree of Death is the possibility for renewed life. The tree that is barren in the winter comes into bud in the spring.

In the most famous biblical reference to bones, Ezekiel prophesies over the dry bones of Israel's slain:

> Then said He to me, "Prophesy unto the spirit, prophesy, Son of Adam, and say to the Spirit: Thus says the Lord YHVH: Come from the four winds, O spirit, and breathe upon these slain, that they may live." So I prophesied as He commanded me, and the spirit came into them, and they lived, and stood up upon their feet, an exceeding great host.

> Then He said to me, "Son of Adam, these bones are the whole house of Israel; behold, they say, 'Our bones are dried up, and our

hope is lost; we are clean cut off.' Therefore prophesy, and say unto them: Thus says the Lord YHVH: Behold, I will open your graves and cause you to come up out of your graves, O My people, and I will bring you into the land of Israel.

"And you shall know that I am the Lord when I have opened your graves and caused you to come up out of your graves, O My people. And I will put My spirit in you and you shall live, and I will place you in your own land; and you shall know that I YHVH have spoken and acted, said YHVH."

Summary: Bazak Eighteen to Bazak Twenty

After the death of Joseph, the four hundred years of servitude foretold to Abraham begin. Near the end of that period, the decrees issued against the Hebrews grow ever more severe.

A child is born to a Hebrew woman, placed in an ark and hidden among the reeds at the river bank to save its life. He is raised by the daughter of Pharaoh and named Mosheh, or Moses. When he is grown, he kills an Egyptian who is beating a Hebrew.

Moses flees to Midian and works as a shepherd for a priest, Jethro, who gives him his daughter for a wife. In Bazak Nineteen he names their son Gershom for "I have been a stranger there."

Moses' life is transformed in the desert when he hears the voice of God from a bush that burns but is not consumed. He is told he is a *shaliach,* a Messsenger of the Lord, an angel. He is to go to Pharaoh and free God's people from bondage. *Mi anochi,* he cries. Who am I to go to Pharaoh? And God says to him, as God says to each of us, the words of the sustaining covenant, *Ehyeh imach.* " I will be with you."

Bazak Twenty-One
בזק כ"א השם
Ha'Shem - The Name

ויאמר משה אל־האלהים הנה אנכי בא אל־בני ישראל
ואמרתי להם אלהי אבותיכם שלחני אליכם ואמרו־לי
מה־שמו מה אמר אלהם ויאמר אלהים אל משה
אהיה אשר אהיה ויאמר כה תאמר לבני ישראל אהיה
שלהני אליכם...יהוה אלהי אבתיכם אלהי אברהם
אלהי יצחק ואלהי יעקב שלחני אליכם
זה־שמי לעלם וזה זכרי לדר דר

*And Moses said to God, "Behold I come to the chil-
dren of Israel and say to them, 'The God of your fa-
thers sent me to you,' and they shall say to me,
'What's his name?' What shall I say to them?" And
God said to Moses, "I shall be that which shall be."
And He said, "Thus shall you say to the children of
Israel, 'Ehyeh sent me to you...YHVH, God of your
fathers, God of Abraham, God of Isaac, and God of
Jacob sent me to you. This is My Name forever, and
in It remember Me for all generations.*
—Exodus 3:13-15

Commentary, Bazak Twenty-one
יהוה
Ha'Shem - The Name

Jerusalem

There is a small train on a narrow track that connects Jerusalem with Tel Aviv.

The train, a relic of the British occupation of Palestine, has high, narrow sides rounded at the top. In the early morning, Arab families en route to Ramallah, a Chasid and his boy on their way to Kfar Chabad, make up the early morning, mostly empty, passenger list. The train clatters and sways through the hills of Jerusalem, following the track of a stream. The hills and sky and small settlements are dotted with sheep and donkeys carrying small loads, followed by young shepherds.

Weaving through the condos and minarets of Jerusalem's outskirts, the train turns so sharply the locomotive can be seen from the passenger windows, steam billowing from the stack, before plunging into the rocks and deep gorges that open on to the Judean wilderness that swarmed with Jerusalem's enemies, all these three thousand years. In this land God revealed His Presence in ways previously unknown in the world and the radiance of that revelation fuels the dreams of billions of human beings to this day. And brooding over Jerusalem and the world is the awesome Name of God.

In the Name of God

When I ended the long Exile of my fathers and returned to Israel, I went to a kibbutz in the north, near Beth Shean, where the Philistines fastened the headless bodies of King Saul and his son, Jonathan, to the city walls three thousand years ago. I went up to the holy city of Jerusalem, where the Romans broke down the walls and sacked the Temple, two thousand years ago. And I prayed with the Bratslavers and placed notes in the Western Wall, and walked the dusty streets of Jerusalem.

Jerusalem seems risen from another planet — the light and sky and bright air, cool on its little mountain. The Old City of Jerusalem has sun-baked incense deep in its stones and there are the prayers of holy men and women in every crevice, prayers from Christians and Moslems and Jews.

This place, now teeming with taxis and buses, the skyline punctuated by giant construction cranes, was built by King David to house the Name of God

> And David arose and went with all
> the people that were with him from
> Baalim Judah to bring up from there the
> Ark of God, to which the Name is attached
> even the Name of YHVH of armies,
> [the Name] that sits upon the cherubim.

Now, King David's palace, the Temple, the Ark and the cherubim are gone, carried off. And what of the Name?

Once I found myself in my grandfather's shul in Tiktin, a little shtetl in Poland near the Russian border. There, in August 1941, all 1407 Jewish souls were taken to the square across from the massive Catholic church, the statue of Czarnieki in the square pointing across to the women and men and small children. They were beaten by peasants armed with axes and farm implements as German Nazis looked on. The bloodied survivors were marched to the forest at Topoucho, killed, and thrown into a pit. Today that shul is a Polish tourist attraction, one of the last synagogues standing from those dark times. Painted on the *bimah*, the podium from which the Torah is read, is יהוה, the Tetragrammaton, the YHVH that stands for the Name of God.

But was not God in the pit and in the streets, in the whip and in the terror? God was very near, in each shallow breath and panicked heartbeat; in the guttural screams and savage barking was heard the Voice of God, and in the Kaddish and the Shema did the beaten, murdered Jews still call upon the Name of God.

In all that great stretch of time, and for millennia before King David came up to Jerusalem, the Hebrew tribes have told the story of Creation of the world, of living souls, and death and rebirth in the presence of the Creator. They told these stories around their desert campfires and in their towns and walled cities. Christians and Moslems have woven those stories into the center of their lives. And always, at the heart of each story, stands the awesome Name of God.

God's Name

This is the forbidden mystery. The Name -- *ha'Shem* -- may not be spoken, may not be written. Who has forbidden it? The Hebrew priests took pains to protect the Name, to limit its use, to disguise it. The Name was potent and could be used to practice magic and that would be a desecration. And yet YHVH commanded "In it remember Me."

It is said that once a year the High Priest in Jerusalem would enter the Holy of Holies in the Temple, on Yom Kippur, the Day of Atonement. He would enter between the wings of the flaming Cherubs over the Ark and go behind the Curtain of the Ark. When he came out he would utter the Name of God.

And then it is said that, over the years, the Jews forgot the Name. And simply referred to YHVH as *HaShem,* the Name, or *Adonai,* Lord.

In these days, it may be said that many Jews no longer even remember there was a Name and simply borrow the generic term for God used by the people among whom they live.

And yet the Name is central. At the crown of the Hebrew religion stands the Name. So the Ancients, to make sure that those searching for the Name would be able to find it again, left a mark, broke off a branch along the trail.

YHVH. Yod-Hay-Vav-Hay, the Tetragrammaton, is itself the marker left in the sand to point our way back to the Name.

We need it now. Our hearts are broken and we are howling in the wilderness, lost in darkness.

There is a way, in these days, to find the Name of God and to attach our lives to that Name.

Maimonides said, "The precept at the root of all the commandments and the principle of faith have their source in this basic idea -- 'to know that there is a God. I would say that 'to know' means that our conviction of the existence of God should become a constant and continuous awareness of the reality of God, a level of consciousness never marred by inattention. "

To achieve that "constant and continuous awareness of the reality of God" requires us to focus on the Name.

When we name something we acknowledge its nature, we participate in bringing it into our being. "And whatever Adam called every living creature, that was its name."

The Angel asked Jacob, "Why do you ask me my name? " Rashi cites *Genesis Rabbah* to explain the Angel's inability to say his name: "We have no fixed names. Our names change depending on the service we are commanded to carry out and the errand with which we are charged."

The functional name, such as Mosheh, the Rescuer, or Asaph, the Carried Off, is a condition of those bearing the name, a description of their role in the World. What function did the Hebrews find in the ineffable Name?

"I place my Angel before you to guard you on
the way and to bring you into the place
which I have made ready. Do not defy him,
for he will not forgive your trespasses for I
place my Name in him."

The Angel placed before the Children of Israel is Moses or Mosheh. Name, in Hebrew is spelled with a Shin (ש) and Mem (מ). Within the name Mosheh is a Shin (ש) and a Mem (מ). Even more significantly, the name Mosheh (משה) reversed, is identical to HaShem, The Name, an honorific used in referring to YHVH.

In Bazak Twenty-one, found in the third chapter of Exodus, the biblical book known in Hebrew as "The Book of Names," YHVH tells the Angel Mosheh His Name. This is a revelation, this evolution from God Almighty (El Shaddai) to the God of Be-ing who promises

Mosheh, "For I shall be with you (*ki-ehyeh imach*). "
Mosheh then says:

> "Behold I come to the children of Israel and
> say to them 'The God (Elohay) of your fa-
> thers has sent me to you,' and they shall say
> to me, 'What is his Name?' What shall I say
> to them? "
> And God (Elohim) said to Mosheh," I shall
> be that which shall be (*Ehyeh asher Ehyeh*)."
> And He said, "Thus shall you say to the chil-
> dren of Israel, 'Ehyeh has sent me to you...
> YHVH, God (Elohay) of your fathers, God
> (Elohay) of Abraham, God (Elohay) of Isaac
> and God (Elohay) of Jacob sent me to you. '
> This is My Name forever and in It remember
> Me for all generations. "

In Bazak Twenty-one we can see both the function of
The Name — Be-ing — and the disguising form that
may be used to refer to It —YHVH. Elohim and Elohay
are generic allusions to God but do not contain God's
name, do not convey any attributes of God. By using the
Tetragrammaton, YHVH, immediately after the Torah
discloses the Name EHYEH. Using YHVH to stand for
EHYEH is one means for Ancient Hebrew scribes to
establish the code. Embedded in YHVH is the Name
EHYEH, from the Hebrew verb, היה, *hayah*, be.

The shortened form of the Name, Yah, was incorpo-
rated within personal names, such as JeremiYAH, frequently replacing the name of the Canaanite deity El
(e.g., Ezeki-EL). This same abbreviated form is used in
prayer and hymns of praise — as in Praise Yah, *Hallelu-
Yah* — to this day.

Rashi says the phrase, "This is My Name forever, lacks a vav in the word forever (*l'olam*). [Normally it would be spelled Ayin-Vav-Lamed-Mem.] so that it may be read *l'alam* [Ayin-Lamed-Mem] and it would mean, 'this is My Name which is to be concealed' to suggest: Conceal it (this divine Name), so it shall not be read exactly as it is written...."

Be-ing, the Name of God

Concealment of the Name and its underlying essence, offered as a memorial from generation to generation, contributes to confusion and delusion today, making the Name of God a trivial matter for which the generic Adonai or God is easily substituted.

The danger in these times is not in revealing the Name of God but in so conspiring to conceal it that such variations as Yahwe and Jehovah are used, presumably representing a sounding out of the Tetragrammaton, yet stripping the Name of its awesome direct meaning.

Ehyeh — Be-ing.

It is through the Name itself that we can enter the mystery of Creation, for it is not only in Be-ing but in the particular nature of the future (I Shall Be) rushing in tumultuous waves through the present moment to crash upon the shores of the past that we live and serve God, that intersection in which we may know God, that we may attach ourselves to God.

Ehyeh is Creation itself, the on-rushing explosive force we see all around us, streaming away beyond the speed of light in combustible starry formations, in the crucible of the universe, creating, sustaining, destroying all in its path in implacable majesty.

To meditate on Be-ing, to be constantly aware of the present streaming moment, is to know YHVH. Near the end of *The Hebrew Book of the Dead*, at the day of his own death, the Angel Mosheh will reveal the Great Commandment that brings this awareness to each soul with each breath and pulse of life.

Summary:
Bazak Twenty-two to Bazak Twenty- three

After a series of plagues called down on Egypt, the children of Israel leave Egypt on the night of the Passover when the Angel of Death kills all the firstborn in the Land of Egypt except the children of Israel.

Before leaving, Moses takes up the bones of Joseph and carries them with him.

The Israelites make their first camps before the *Yam Sof,* the Sea of Ending. (See Appendix B.)

The chariots of Pharaoh pursue the children of Israel. Moses lifts up his rod and divides the sea, revealing the dry earth below. The children of Israel cross on firm ground, but when Pharaoh's chariots pursue, the waters roll back upon the Egyptians.

Reflection: Coming to the World of Yetzirah

On the full moon, as the tides are drawn away from the land, at the time of the low tide, the bones of Asaph are carried up from his ancient grave. He is beginning his soul's journey across the wilderness to be reborn in the Promised Land.

The staging area is the house of the god Thum, the treasure city of Pi-Thum in the district of Thuku, a city of booths and tents sprawling at the edge of the great wilderness.

Despite the cold, bright moonlight, across the Yam Sof, the Sea of Ending, the wilderness is dim and hidden by dust in the night. The smell of the salt sea rises on a light breeze and there are sounds of water lapping at the banks.

From Pi-Thum the Hebrews move on, closer to the Sea, to the string of lakes by Pi-haChiroth, a larger settlement crowded with low houses made of mud brick and straw. Pi-haChiroth is set near a string of brackish lakes leading to the Sea of Ending. A larger caravan tenting ground and an open market, a *shuk* with tables and rough shelters, borders the area claimed by the Hebrews.

Although it is already dark, there is activity in the area near the animal pens. Camels are snuffling and restless as dark figures bundle and unbundle burdens. In the night there are dark whispers and occasional shouts and laughter.

Two structures mark this place. The great lookout tower of Migdol is here. Erected by Rameses to defend the Lower Kingdom against incursions by marauding bands, the tower is now a landmark. Migdol has become became a high signpost in a flat world, a beacon used by dusty traders and nomadic tribes to mark the approach to Pi-haChiroth, where water and markets — and Pharoah's guards — await travelers entering the kingdom.

Facing the lookout tower is Pi-haChiroth's other monument, a dark, grim statue of the Lord of the North, Baal-Tzephon, broad and burnished black with a golden sun disk behind his horned head, towering over the low desert brick buildings. The Baal-Tzephon is the local deity, ranking only slightly lower than Pharaoh himself among the villagers. A collection of bones and broken pottery is scattered around the idol's altar. The priests of Baal-Tzephon can be dimly seen preparing the morning offerings.

In this place rest the *atzmot*, the *bones* of Asaph, in his ark, in the company of his cohort and the Angel of the Lord. It is Asaph's last stop in the World of Assiyah.

Before dawn a great cloud of dust rises in the distance and the sound of thunder rumbles in the sands. The adobe buildings shake and the Baal Tzephon seems to rock from side to side in glee. It is the sound of chariots and horses now mixed with loud drumming and hoarse shouts. The Hebrews cry out to the Angel Mosheh in fear of Pharaoh's power.

The Angel rises and with a silent word places a veil of darkness between the Hebrews and Pharaoh's legions. Pharaoh's legions are of the World of Assiyah and are not permitted to enter the Wilderness beyond the edge of the water. For this is the Yam Sof, the Sea of Ending that opens onto Yetzirah, the World of Formation, the dominion of angels. Moses turns and stretches out his hands and the winds rise from the east to separate the waters.

Lit by the last cold light of the desert moon, the waters separate to make way for this soul leaving the World of Assiyah, leaving to enter the realm of angels. The earth uncovered by the receding waters is strangely dry and fresh, fragrant as in the beginning.

The Hebrews with the bones of Asaph cross the Yam Sof on dry earth, the newly opened virgin soil. The waters of the Sea are a wall to them on their right and on their left.

In the breaking dawn, behind them, across the Sea of Ending the children of Israel hear a clamor at the Gates of Assiyah, even at the great tower of Migdol. There are shouts and curses from the armies of the world, but the walls of water slam shut and a terrifying Angel stands at the Gate to Yetzirah, guarding the passage of this soul, his rod become a flashing sword.

Soon there is only silence across the seas reflecting glints of red and gold in the first morning watch.

Before the exultant Hebrews there are the dim outlines of a new world. The heat of the day has not yet risen and yet there is no cold in the air, no chill in the desert rocks resting on the sandy earth. The air is still and quiet. Low bushes and distant ridges of barely visible mountains roll out to the far horizon in a cloud of blue shadow.

The Angel and the bones of Asaph and the children of Israel have come beyond the furthest reaches of the World of Assiyah to cross the watery border into the Wilderness, into the World of Yetzirah where clothes do not rot and food grows not from the ground but falls from the heavens. While trade and procreation, lust and appetite are the work of Assiyah, in this world they will find neither markets nor sex nor birth nor death.

This is the great wilderness of Yetzirah, the place where souls are renewed. In this world rumblings come not from the drumming of horses' hooves on sand but in thunder over the mountains, in the voices of fearsome angels.

Far off, beyond the bitter waters of Marah, beyond the well watered oasis Elim with its seventy palm trees, lie the peaks of Sinai and the work of redemption.

And at the furthest end of the vast wilderness, the sweet waters of the River Jordan, the Sea of Descent, lap the banks of the land flowing with milk and honey. There the ancient city of *Gilgal*, the Wheel, welcomes travelers back into life in the flesh. There, in the Canaanite village of Shechem, under the Sun shining over the

Holy Land, the open field of his father awaits the bones of Asaph.

Summary:
Bazak Twenty-four to Bazak Twenty-five

After wanderings and trials, the children of Israel, led by the Angel Moses bearing the bones of Joseph, arrive at Mount Sinai and, in Bazak Twenty-five, receive the Ten Commandments.

Moses enters the thick darkness to receive the tablets while the children of Israel tremble and stand off below, witnessing the thunderings and lightnings, the voice of the shofar and the smoking mountain.

Before the Commandments are transmitted to the Hebrew tribes, God issues the first judgment and ordinances by which the children of Israel shall live. The first among those is Bazak Twenty-six, the judgment concerning freedom and the Hebrew slave.

Bazak Twenty-Six
בזק כ"ו העבד
Ha'Eved - The Slave

כי תקנה עבד עברי שש שנים יעבד ובשבעת
יצא לחפשי חנם אם־בגפו יבו בגפו יצא אם־בעל
אשה הוא ויצה אשתו עמו אם־אדניו יתן־לי אשה
וילדה־־לו בנים או בנות האשה וילדיה תהיה
לאדניה והוא יצא בגפו ואם־אמר יאמר העבד
אהבתי את־אדני את־אשתי ואת־בני לא אצא חפשי
והגישו אדניו אל־האלהים והגישו אל־הדלת או
אל־המזוזה ורצע אדניו את־אזנו במרצע
ועבד לעלם

*If you buy a Hebrew slave, six years he shall serve
and in the seventh he shall go free without payment.
If single (in his body) he came, single he shall go out.
If married, he shall go out with his wife. If his master has given him a wife and she bears him sons or
daughters, the wife and children shall be her master's and he shall go out single. But if the slave speaks
saying, "I love my lord, my wife, my children I will*

not go out free," then the master shall bring him be-
fore God and bring him to the door or the doorpost
and the master shall bore his ear with an awl and he
shall serve him forever.

—Exodus 21:2-6

Commentary: Bazak Twenty-six
עבד עברי
Ha'Eved — The Slave

Thunder cracks the mountain top. Thick smoke in a fiery plume darkens the sky. Lightning flashes illuminate the dense cloud cover as the deafening wail of the ram's horn blares long and urgent shrieks in the night. Sharp trumpet blasts pierce the thunderbolts and shake the mountain. The ground where the Hebrews stand undulates with violent waves as a sea ripped by hurricane. The whole top of the mountain is a furnace vomiting black smoke as the devouring fire storm descends on the peaks and the blasts of the ram's horn, long and deafening, slowly fade.

With a series of spasms the earth settles and the mountain grows quiet. The sky clears. The Angel descends from the mountain with the ten words he heard on the mountain top, the words that open *Anochi YHVH*, I am Ehyeh. I am your God.

After Moses tells the children of Israel all the Commandments, the camp of the Hebrews grows still, the air charged with fire, the ground littered with ash and stone. In this aftermath of the revelation on the mountain, the statutes and ordinances flowing from these Commandments, are given to the Hebrews.

The ordinance that stands first among all is Bazak Twenty-six, *The Slave.* It is the first rule and in it are all the Commandments found. After seven years of servitude, says Bazak Twenty-six, the slave must be set free. What is to be done with the slave who refuses freedom for love of his wife and child?

"His master shall pierce his ear with an awl and he shall remain his slave forever."

Not yet cleared of life in Assiyah, still far from reincarnation across the River of Descent, Asaph and the children of Israel are warned of the awl in the ear, for slavery is the common fate of the mud man, the living soul in a human body.

We have seen in the early *bazakim* how the *Nefesh Chayah,* the living soul, rises from the primal mud, the song of the Spirit in its ears, to stumble off into a life of confusion, beauty, pain and despair.

In all its wanderings, this Spirit burning in the flesh, this stranger in a strange land, lives as a slave to its desires, until it breaks free and enters the wilderness.

Is not Asaph himself the Hebrew slave? As a boy, he is a slave to vanity, ignorance, passion, a slave to dreams, and to power. He is sold as a slave to serve his master Potiphar in the house of Pharaoh. He serves Pharoah. It is only after Asaph the slave is laid to rest in a coffin in Egypt, only when he is lifted up from the pit, does he begin his true quest for freedom, for *chofesh,* in the desert wilderness of Yetzirah, the World of Formation.

The Eleventh Commandment

Mosheh lifts up the bones of Asaph and carries them through the Gates to the Sea of Ending, carries him into the desert wilderness, to begin the process of *chofshi*, becoming free. While at the base of the still smoking mountain, with receding echoes of thunder in the desert air, the Hebrews wait to receive the first rule, the Eleventh Commandment of YHVH.

Thou shalt be free. The first rule is to be free.

All the rivers of souls that have poured into Asaph stand at the foot of the mountain to hear the Ten Commandments of freedom. You shall no longer be a slave to desire, to power, to false gods, to masters. You shall be free to serve YHVH with all your heart, free in the Sabbath of Sabbaths, free of desire and deceit.

What is the Nature of this Freedom?

Who does not love his wife and children? Who would go to his freedom leaving his wife and children in bondage? And yet we are so commanded.

"It is here," writes Reb Nachman Tiktinner, HaRanit, in *Shaarei Melech* "that the voyaging soul must burn off the last remnants of its fleshly body. In the story of the

Hebrew slave, The Torah places unconditional freedom first among the ordinances of YHVH."

The Rebbe wrote:

> *There are Four Worlds*
> *and to each there is a gate.*
> *Beyond each gate lies a sea*
> *and across each sea a wilderness*
> *leading to each World.*
>
> *This World rests on the Ten Words*
> *uttered by the Holy One on Sinai.*
> *Together the Ten Words [de]mand*
> *freedom of the Nefesh*
>
> *Freedom to love YHVH*
> *Freedom from Desire*
> *Freedom from Power*
> *Freedom from Fear*
> *Freedom to hear His voice*
> *Ehyeh is that which Is.*

And What is Freedom?

The first rule given by the Angel Mosheh at the Mountain of the Lord points the path for the Soul in the Midbar. To be naked, to be holy for God is holy, to be free of all servitude is just the practical application of the First Commandment.

Anochi, even I, YHVH, am your God, who has brought you out of the Land of Bondage, the House of Servants. You shall have no other Gods before me, neither Mammon nor your most loved ones. Abraham understood that as he prepared to sacrifice his son. Life is mine, says God.

There is only one God, the life behind all these illusions, the core Spirit.

So Great a Prisoner Are We

As in a dream, YHVH bursts into human consciousness through the Torah. Let us not ask if God is there, but if we are truly *here*. The architecture of the Worlds, the geometry of our slavery, is revealed in the Torah.

As we stand on Earth, looking out at an unbounded universe, all the visible worlds are streaming, exploding away from us. Wherever we stand, each of us is the very center of the universe. The objects most distant from us move away fastest, just as we move away from those objects. In this World of Assiyah, our sense that we are the center of this unfolding spectacle is our ultimate prison.

The weight of matter bends space, slows time, and folds the Universe back in upon itself, upon us.

Imprisoned within a physical body, on a small planet in a desolate solar system set on a distant arm of a remote spiral galaxy, we live our days in the company of prisoners. As far as we can see, our prison walls extend outward.

And even if we could reach the nearest neighboring star — in a journey that far exceeds the total journeys of this planet Earth around the Sun in its billions of years of existence — even if we could make that extraordinary leap, we would still be at the center of a world exploding away from us, equally, in every direction.   So shackled a prisoner are we.

And yet, in an instant, we shed these bones and enter other universes where a different level of Creation is at work. We enter a World that not only borders our own, but encompasses it, powers it through the Light of *Ayn Sof,* the Eternal Light that filters through the membranes separating the Worlds. In an instant, we are free!

We are commanded to be free even while we are within our bodies of mud.

The nature of the curtain, separating the Light of *Ayn Sof* from each World, the curtain separating the Worlds, is like an amniotic membrane that permits fluids to pass from the mother to the fetal child. The curtain permits reduced potencies of Light to filter through the Worlds. We may be slaves but we are surrounded by Radiance and through the body itself can we come to know the Presence of YHVH in all our days.

The curtain that hung before the Holy of Holies when the Temple stood in Jerusalem today lies within our hearts, separating the holy from the profane, freedom from slavery.

Come, see the dance of slave and master.

Shall the slave be a master? This bazak is addressed to the master at the moment of purchase, at the moment of decision. *Ki tikneh...*when you shall buy a slave. At this moment, there is still time to choose before the mask sticks to the face, the costume to the body. To have a slave means to be a master. And to be a slave means to have a master. Each requires the other as darkness requires light.

After six years the slave may renounce his freedom. At the end of six years, it is the slave who becomes the master, it is the slave who can choose to renounce his freedom and remain, supported by his master.

Is Asaph a master or slave? Surely Asaph was a slave to the Ishmaelites, a slave to Potiphar the Egyptian overseer, a slave to Pharaoh. And even as the *Baal Cholem,* the Master of Dreams, master of all Egypt, second only to the Pharaoh he remained a slave to worldly power.

Asaph himself, as he grows old, recognizes his dual state and yearns for his freedom. Reunited with his brothers, he returns the bones of his father to the Promised Land, the land bought from Hamor, the Shechemite, in Canaan. Near his own death, Asaph commands that his soul, too, be carried up out of the Lower Kingdom and be taken across the river into the Promised Land that he might fulfill the Covenant and be *chofesh*, free at last.

It can be seen, says Rabbi Nachman Tiktinner, Ha-Ranit, "freedom is the single task of the enslaved soul. It is only in the state of *chofesh* that the Spirit, freed of its mud body, can cross the Fire at the Gate and return to its source. "

And if the slave refuses *chofesh*, refuses his freedom, for the sake of his wife and his child, He shall have his ear bored to the doorpost and be a slave forever.

And Why the Doorpost

The freedom from Egypt, the Land of Bondage, is only the beginning of freedom from servitude. Slavish desire after cucumbers and fleshpots, the desires of the belly, are finally no different than love for a wife and child, the desires of the heart. This is the truth that will free the Soul from its shell. (In Sephirotic terms, the rigor of God's *Din*, Judgment, is required to neutralize the mercy of God's *Chesed*, Lovingkindness.)

Blood of the sacrificed lamb was dashed on the lintel and the doorpost that first Passover night. Between the bloody doorposts, Israel moved out of slavery to cross the *Yam Sof*, to come up to the Mountain of God in the wilderness.

It is the bloody doorpost, the *mezzuzah*, that stands as witness to the Exodus to freedom. It is through bloody portals that we are born anew.

And, to this day, is not the doorpost, the *mezzuzah*, the place where Jews are commanded to affix the implacable words of the Shema: "Hear O Israel YHVH your God, YHVH is One. You shall love the Lord with all your heart and all your might...." Not "you shall love the

Lord as well as your children, your wife, your work, your things." In seeking a balance, we twist in the winds of Assiyah all our life.

And Why the Ear?

It is the ear that heard the Word on Sinai, say the rabbis, and soon, in the shadow of Sinai, it will be from those ears that the gold rings shall be taken to make the golden calf, that illusion of security that stood between the Hebrews and YHVH. That still stands in our hearts.

Karen and the Awl

Since we daily sacrifice our freedom and life for the sake of our children and loved ones, how can we reconcile the requirement to be free with life in Assiyah?

Rashi says this rule can be found in Leviticus, the third book of the Torah: "For it is to Me that the Israelites are servants. They are My servants, whom I freed from the land of Bondage. I the Lord your God." We are servants to nothing less than Be-ing.

In my own life I have had my ear securely bored to the doorpost. I lived as a slave, came before God and said I love my wife and my children. I will not go free. And then my wife, Karen, died. Surely my pathetic longing for her jingling presence in our house, the space I made for her each night on our bed, her photographs and paintings hung from each wall, the grieving — was all that not in the service of strange gods?

She made *aliyah* and crossed over the Sea of Ending. In a stroke, in an awful, abrupt departure, neither our children nor I could any longer make offerings on the altar of her love. We could remember its sweet incense and look with marvel at the stains of dried blood around the smoke blackened stones littered with the sacrificial bones of days burnt and gone forever. But of her curls and light step there were none.

In those dark days after she died, I would wash the morning dishes, detach myself from the doorpost, and go forth into the dull morning, an awl dangling firmly from my ear.

One day, I returned home to find our young son asleep, home from school, feverish with a sore throat, in need of care. My heart leaped in me, I returned to life, a willing Servant again. Does not the holy Spirit of YHVH twist in the feverish body of a child?

Finally, the only wisdom is the wisdom of the heart.

The only service is the service of love.

Summary:
Bazak Twenty-seven to Bazak Thirty-two

After issuing the ordinances, God says His angel goes before the children of Israel to bring them into the Promised Land. "Obey him for My Name (Shin-Mem) is in him." God calls Moses up to receive the stone tablets with the teachings and commandments.

When Moses is delayed on Mount Sinai, the Hebrews panic and ask Aaron to make them a god to go before them. Aaron makes them an idol using gold from their earrings, which he casts into a mold to make a molten calf. Aaron then builds an altar before the calf and the people worship.

Moses comes down from the mountain and shatters the tablets at the foot of the mountain and destroys the golden calf. He accuses Aaron of bringing a great sin upon the people. Moses intercedes for the Israelites before God's wrath. God promises to bring the guilty to account for their sin.

Moses asks if he may see God and is told in Bazak Thirty-one "You cannot see My face, for man may not see Me and live." He places Moses in the *nikrat tzur,* a cleft in the rock, where he is shielded by God's hand until he passes. Thus he may see God's back but not God's face. (See Commentary on the cleft of the rock in Bazak Forty.)

After this epiphany, God orders Moses to return to Mount Sinai with two new tablets to receive the words that were on the first tablets. In Bazak Thirty-two, drawn from the Book of Leviticus, God tells the priests what must be done to atone for sin.

If the anointed priest is guilty of sin so blame falls upon the people, a bull of the herd without blemish must be offered. Aaron, the high priest, was guilty of such a sin. And if the whole community of Israel is guilty, a bull of the herd shall be offered. The whole community worshipped the Golden Calf.

God has withdrawn from the community of Israel. Now there is no cloud by day, no pillar of fire by night. The tribes do not move from the base of the Mountain.

Moses prepares a sacrificial offering before the Tent of Meeting that he has set up outside the camp. This is what the Lord commanded. The High Priest Aaron and his sons Nadav and Abihu (their names mean "Willing" and "He is my father") are bathed and commanded by Moses to remain inside the Tent of Meeting for seven days of purification to make expiation

Moses tells Aaron to come forward to the altar and sacrifice his sin offering and his burnt offering and make expiation for himself and the people. The offerings are slaughtered and laid upon the altar, but Aaron's offerings are not accepted, and no fire comes forth from the Lord.

Then Moses and Aaron retire to the Tent of Meeting to meditate and pray. When they return they bless the people and their offering is accepted.

Bazak Thirty-Three
בזק ל"ג אש זרה
Aysh Zarah — Strange Fire

ותצא אש מלפני יהוה ותאכל על־המזבח את־
העלה ואת־החלבים וירא כל־העם וירנו
ויפלו על־פניהם ויקחו בני־אהרן
נדב ואביהוא איש מחתתו
ויתנו בהן אש וישימו עליה קטרת ויקריבו
לפני יהוה אש זרה אשר לו צוה אתם
ותצא אש מלפני יהוה ותאכל אותם וימתו
לפני יהוה ויאמר משה אל־אהרן הוא אשר־
דבר יהוה לאמר בקרבי אקדש ועל־פני כל־
העם אכבד וידם אהרן

Fire came forth from before YHVH and ate the burnt offering and the fat offering on the altar and all the people saw and were astonished and fell on their faces. Then the sons of Aaron, Nadav and Abihu, each took his firepan and put in it fire and spread on it incense and they offered strange fire before YHVH which he had not commanded them and there came forth fire from before YHVH and ate them and they died before YHVH. And Moses said to Aaron, "This is what YHVH spoke saying, 'By those who sacrifice themselves to me shall I be shown holy and sanctified before all the people.'" And Aaron was silent. — Leviticus 9:24, 10:1-3

Commentary: Bazak Thirty-Three
אש זרה
Aysh Zarah - Strange Fire

There are many ways for the body to suffer. There is but one way for the soul. The Mud Man can suffer cuts and burns, swelling, shriveling, broken bones, and beaten flesh. The Soul suffers only from distance from God — exile, lost in the blackness of time without hope for light.

The Mud Man, burning in the burning of its days, dies but once and disintegrates. The Soul lives forever, crosses the Sea of Ending and enters the Wilderness to be reborn in the Wheel, in Gilgal, descending into flesh across the river.

In *The Hebrew Book of the Dead*, the Nefesh Chayah, the Soul in Mud, the living human being, walks the world, dies, and is stripped of its flesh and earthly ties to be set free. This moment of release comes at the foot of the mountain, in the time of Strange Fire.

Death Valley

Once, living in a tent in Death Valley, with scattered household items cluttering up much of two neighboring campsites, I set out to Titus Mountain to see if the prophet Isaiah would bring me a vision of God.

Come, hear. This is a true story.

I drove up to the mountain in my blue Chevy pickup. When I got to a likely spot near the peak, I turned off the road and hiked a short way up the jutting rocks to find a place to sit and read the Book of Isaiah and wait for the desert sunset and a direct vision of God.

The light started to fail before I got to the opening lines of chapter 40:

> *Nachamu, Nachamu, ami*
> Comfort you, comfort you, My people.

I thought I would pitch my tent and light a candle to await the full night thick with low and moving stars of light. The desert wind grew stronger, the darkening night, colder.

Unable to drive a stake into the hard ground, I tied off the ends of my tent to a creosote bush, but the rising wind blew it right out. It grew darker and I could not read and had no shelter and no light.

Below, I saw the darkness cross the desert floor, the dying light in the sky, the blue and dark gray shadows settling around my failed tent. As I say, my bottom grew cold, my crossed legs numb. There was no moon that night. I got back into my pickup and drove down to a hotel parking lot in the Valley and read awhile before crawling into the back of the truck and fell asleep until dawn.

Those were the actions of a fool. I saw my own clown self climbing over the crest of a desert dune, face black with fatigue, shredded little tent and torn book in hand, stumbling back to the campsite. And the security of coffee.

I was a greater fool than I knew. I had been to a holy place, but my aggressive need for a specific revelation, and my body's demand for comfort, blinded me to the burning world swirling around my head.

Thus too have I passed many times over that most holy place in *The Hebrew Book of the Dead*, this bazak that appears in Leviticus, the third book of the Torah. Dazzled and impatient, following the dictates of my cramped body, my various appetites, in haste I missed Strange Fire, this most sacred text. *Aysh Zarah* is the continental divide of the desert wilderness, the intersection where the slave becomes free and the passage to the Promised Land, stalled by the sin of the golden calf, is resumed.

At the Foot of the Mountain

The events of Strange Fire, *Aysh Zarah,* occur at the foot of Mount Sinai.

The events leading up to *Aysh Zarah* tell the story of a soul cringing in the wilderness, fearful and doubtful, looking back, over its shoulder. Brought before the mountain of YHVH, the soul hears the awesome sounds of Revelation, the blowing of the shofar and the fire in the mountain at the giving of the law. And, later, the soul watches as the Angel Mosheh enters the cloud and ascends the Mountain to receive the Word of YHVH.

Moses is up on the mountain for forty days and below the children of Israel are lost, abandoned to their fears. They find in Aaron, the brother of Moses, a willing accomplice. To gladden our hearts, remember the good times, let us build a golden calf and a fire so we may sing and dance. And Aaron takes their gold earrings and melts them down to make an idol, and they dance.

And when the Angel carrying the Tablets of the Testimony descends the mountain to bring the Word to the children of Israel, he hears a boisterous sound. Joshua accompanying him says, "There is a noise of war in the camp."

What Joshua hears in the dance around the golden calf is the death cry of the spirit in the flesh, the terrible longing for the material world, for the remembered pleasures of its own Mud boundaries, the agonized look back at the life left behind.

The Nefesh, in the shrouded darkness of its garments of flesh, rises to follow the golden calf made from the golden ear-rings of the Lower Kingdom.

Through the sounds at the base of the mountain, the Angel Mosheh hears not the sounds of war from the camp below but an agonized cry from the peak. Mosheh says:

אין קול ענות גבורה

It is not the voice of power

אין קול ענות חלושה

It is not the voice of defeat

קול ענות אנכי שמע

Hear the anguished voice of *Anochi,* I-AM.

In these few lines from Exodus 32:18 we see human perception and human frailty alongside Divine pain and angelic *devekuth,* clinging to God. *Anochi,* "I am, " is the opening of the Ten Commandments. While Joshua hears the sounds of the children of Israel dancing around the golden calf, Moses listens to his heart and hears the pained voice of *Anochi,* above him at the mountain top.

Back in camp, Moses accuses Aaron of bringing a great sin upon the children of Israel and smashes the Tablets and the golden calf. And still, as the Angel Mosheh, he begs YHVH to forgive the sin. "This people have sinned a great sin and have made them gods of gold," and

YHVH promises, "In the day that I visit, I will visit their sin upon them."

"I shall visit the iniquity of the fathers upon the children," is part of the Second Commandment, the Commandment prohibiting the making of carved images, prohibiting bowing down to them or serving them. What child does not suffer for the sins of his or her father? And what greater barrier can there be to knowing God than worshiping the works of our own hands, our creations, our money, our fame, our position?

In ways unimagined to the children of Israel this promised visitation will clear the sin of the golden calf and open the path to the Promised Land.

The Sin of the Golden Calf

To become a slave to other gods is to sin against YHVH. It is a sin of all the people. This sin is most particularly the sin of the high priest Aaron, who took the molten gold and formed it into a golden calf.

There are specific consquences for this act and, in God's love, a specific path to expiate this sin that is written in the Book of the Levites. For the community there is one atonement:

> And if the whole community of Israel has sinned... ...when the sin through which they incurred guilt becomes known the congregation shall offer a bull of the herd as a sin offering and bring it before the Tent of Meeting. *-Leviticus 4:13*

And for the High Priest there is another.

> And when the anointed priest has incurred
> guilt so that blame falls upon the people, he
> shall offer for the sin of which he is guilty a
> bull of the herd without a blemish as a sin of-
> fering to the Lord. He shall bring the bull to
> the entrance to the Tent of Meeting.
>
> *- Leviticus 4:3*

Two bulls — one for the congregation, one for the
high priest — two young males without blemish are the
sin offering. Assisting in these offerings are the sons of
Aaron, Nadav and Abihu, newly anointed as priests themselves. Abihu, whose name means "He-Is-My-Father, and
Nadav, whose name means "Willing," are both unmar-
ried, without sin, and ritually pure, having fasted and un-
dergone purification for the seven days leading to Aysh
Zarah.

Earlier, YHVH ordered Moses to bring Aaron and his
sons, Nadab and Abihu to the entrance of the Tent of
Meeting and there to wash them with water and conse-
crate them they may serve YHVH as priests. "This, their
anointing, shall serve them for everlasting priesthood
throughout their generations." The generations of Nadav
and Abihu are to be generations of the spirit, only.

Abihu is to become the offering for his father, the
High Priest. Nadav is to become the willing offering for
the community.

This is the law of the sin offering. In the place where
the burnt offering is killed shall the sin offering be
killed before the Lord. It is most holy. *- Levitcus 6:17*

The sin offering for the golden calf was followed by the *olah*, the burnt offering in supplication for the return of God's grace.

"In the Day that I Visit."

Aaron prepares the burnt offering and lays it upon the altar, but no fire comes forth and the offering is not accepted. He retires to the Tent of Meeting to meditate with Moses, and when they return, fire comes down from the heavens. "And the glory of YHVH appeared before all the people."

At that moment, the sons of Aaron "each took his firepan and put in it fire and spread on it incense and they offered strange fire before YHVH."

The Burnt Offering

> And there came forth fire from before YHVH and ate them and they died before YHVH.   - *Leviticus 10.3*

Why were Nadav and Abihu taken as burnt offerings? What is it in our souls that needs burning off, purification through this and no other means? The burnt offering, say the rabbis, is the highest offering for it is consumed entirely.

The burnt offering — the *olah* — is unique among the offerings of the Ancient Hebrews. Unlike the sin and trespass offerings, unlike the meat, drink, heave and wave offerings, it has nothing to do with atonement or forgiveness of sin. The olah is made strictly for renewal and sanctification, renewal of the Covenant of Grace with God.

The "blue light below," says Gershom Scholem in his commentary on the *Zohar*

> (and) the white light above. Israel is the blue light between the material that is burnt and the white light above. The blue light consumes that which is below by rising to the white light above, joining (both) and at that time peace reigns in all the worlds and all together form a unity.

The olah is also know as the *challil*, the whole offering. The Sabbath bread of the Jews, the challah, stands for this offering to this day.

Josef Karo — saint, kabbalist, ascetic of 16th century Safed, and author of the *Shulchan Aruch* that governs portions of Orthodox Jewish practice to this day — wished to be burned at the stake.   In his diaries, he writes of his longing to be burned that he may become clean and pure.

> Consider yourself, therefore, as a perfect burnt-offering and [take care to] be without blemish that might invalidate the sacrifice. For he who is killed by the sword or strangled for the holiness [of God's Name] is like a sin-offering or a trespass-offering (part of which is eaten by the priests) because the flesh remains in this world. But he who is burned for the holiness of God is like a burnt sacrifice which rises wholly upwards.

There came forth fire from before YHVH and ate them and they died before YHVH.

Just as each of us quite literally flares and burns in the absolute zero of deep space, so can we make of our lives, our burning an offering to YHVH, so can we attach ourselves to the Name of God and clear the sin, the blindness, and the fears, of our fathers, our priests, our communities, our selves.

And How Far Upward?

In his translation of the *Zohar,* Daniel Matt offers this story:

> Rabbi El'azar asked Rabbi Shim'on his father, "The bond of *olah* (the burnt offering), bound to the Holy of Holies, lighting up the joining of desire of priests, Levites, and Israel up above — how high does it ascend?"
> He replied, "We have already established this: to Infinity. For all binding and union and wholeness are secreted in the secrecy that cannot be grasped and cannot be known. That includes the desire of all desires. Infinity does not abide being known, does not produce end or beginning.

To end the exile of the Soul, it must be brought near (*karov*) to YHVH.

Karov — Coming Near

Maimonides says *karov*— to approach, to come near — is the act in which an individual approaches another.

> You must hold fast to the principal that there is no difference whether an individual is at

the center of the earth, or, supposing that this
were possible, in the highest part of the ninth
heavenly sphere. For he is not farther off
from God in the one case (here) and no
nearer to Him in the other (there). For nearness to Him, may He be exalted, consists in
apprehending Him; and remoteness from
Him is the lot of him who does not know
Him. And there are very many gradations in
being near to or far away from Him in this
respect.

In *Aysh Zarah, karov* is the critical element in the majestic verse of Leviticus 10:3. The Angel Mosheh approaches his brother, the high priest Aaron, to comfort
him on the loss of his sons. His words of consolation are
few. He reminds Aaron of what YHVH has said,
b'karovay ehkahdaysh — "By those sacrificed to Me shall I
be shown holy." Aaron is to take comfort in the holy mar-
tyrdom of his sons. And Aaron is silent.

Moses then calls two young men to the altar. "*Karvu,*
Come Near, to carry your brothers from the sanctuary."
Over this use of the form, *karov,* a compound wailing
trope is placed in the Torah to extend, sweeten, and high-
light this word. It is as if this rare cantillation marking
was set as a signal, a flare, down through the centuries to
alert the reader that, even though all the Torah is holy,
this is a most holy place.

The word *karov,* the root of "coming near," is also the
root of *korvan,* the offering of the sacrifice. The sacrifice
itself is frequently simply called the *korvan,* for the way of
sacrifice draws the soul of the offerer near God. We require the offering, not God.

114

The Devouring Fire

Nadab and Abihu made the ultimate offering, the offering of their whole spiritual and physical being. It was a sacrifice accepted in the devouring fire.

The fire that comes forth from YHVH accepts the *olah*. Fire (*aysh*) is the transubstantiating medium that proceeds from God, to draw the sacifice near. The Hebrew root of the word *olah* is also the root of *aliyah*, to rise up. Through fire does the offering rise up, transformed, but what of eating?

Achal

Maimonides finds two meanings to the Hebrew word for eating, *achal.* The first is destruction and disappearance and the second is learning, understanding, as in "Come, eat fat meat at the house of Raba," and he quotes from a midrash on the Book of Ecclesiastes that says, "All eating and drinking referred to in this book signify wisdom exclusively." He notes that some say this applies to the Torah.

The eating of the sacrifice, its destruction by fire, represents taking, or accepting, the offering of the soul. The *Nefesh* becomes whole and YHVH is glorified by the willingness of the offering to reenter the Body of God.

By eating the offering, by knowing the body, YHVH signaled acceptance of the sacrifice. In the eating is the body returned to its elements.

The fire that went forth from YHVH brought the nefesh of Nadav and Abihu near (*karov*), that the whole
congregation and Aaron the high priest might draw near
to God.

You shall be holy, for I the Lord am holy is not a commandment. No action is required. It is simply the fundamental spiritual fact of human life.

After the events of *Aysh Zarah* the *Nefesh* begins its
trek, as a free soul, back across the Midbar to the River of
Descent, back into fresh garments of flesh, to do the work
of YHVH.

Strange Fire

What is the Strange Fire offered by Nadab and Abihu?
There was no fire offering in the Tabernacle service. And
the incense in their firepans was the incense of the altar.
So what was it that Nadav and Abihu offered?   It has
been written that they were intoxicated, and it has been
written that they were usurping the role of the high priest.
But the Torah says only that "*they offered strange fire before YHVH which he had not commanded.*"

It was not a prohibited offering, it was an uncom-
manded, willing, and joyful offering. The Strange Fire, is
Aysh Zarah. The offering is the Son of Man, the life of the
unblemished sons sacrified for the sanctification of God's
Name. "By those sacrificed to Me shall I be sanctified."
Nadav and Abihu themselves were the strange fire.

Know this. In Hebrew, man, **אִישׁ** (Aleph-Yod-Shin)
or *Ish* is identical to the word for fire, **אֵשׁ** (Aleph-Shin)
aysh except for the additional Yod found in man.

That Yod (י֜ד), the tenth letter of the Hebrew Alphabet, means "hand" and is composed of the letters Yod (י) and Dalet (ד), which is the fourth letter of the Hebrew alphabet. The numbers 10 and 4 make the number 14 or 1 + 4 which equals 5, the Hebrew letter Hay (ה). Yod-Hay (יה) is the spelling of Yah, a locution for God's Name as in *Hallelu-Yah,* literally, " Praised be Yah." The fire offering made by Nadav and Abihu is the אִישׁ, the God-in-Man, the willing return of the animating spirit to YHVH.

This gematriya reminds us of something we already know. In Man is the fire of God, and are we not quite literally burnt offerings from the beginning? Knowledge of the source of our burning is a source of continual joy.

> *Ivdu ivdu et ha'Shem b'simcha*
> Serve the Lord in gladness
> *Bo l'ifanuf b'rinah*
> Come before the Lord in rejoicing.

Summary:
Bazak Thirty-four — Bazak Thirty-eight

With the return of YHVH to the camp of the Children of Israel, the journey across the Wilderness to freedom, bringing the bones of Joseph to the Promised Land, continues. The Hebrews still exhibit many signs of slavishness, crying for the cucumbers, melons, and leeks of Egypt. Bazak Thirty-four through Bazak Thirty-six reasserts the need for single-minded love of YHVH as the path to freedom.

Approaching Canaan in Bazak Thirty-seven amd Thirty-eight, spies are sent out and return terrified with tales of unconquerable giants in the land. The people beg to return to Egypt. The children of Israel are condemned to forty years of wandering in the desert until they are cleared of slavishness. Between revolt and war, the last of the slaves are gone, rooted out, consumed from the midst of the camp of Israel, and the wanderings cease.

Here, on the plains of Moab, the Angel Mosheh prepares to deliver the Great Commandment that will sustain and guide the Spirit about to descend into the flesh.

Bazak Thirty-Nine
בזק ל"ט הדבר
The Word - Ha'Devar

כי המצוה הזאת אשר אנכי מצבך היום
לא־נפלאת הוא ממך ולא־רחקה הוא לא
בשמים הוא לאמר מי יעלה־לנו השמימה
ויקחה לנו וישמענו אתה ונעשנה ולא־מעבר
לים הוא לאמר מי יעבר־לנו אל־עבר הים
ויקחה לנו וישמענו אתה ונעשנה כי קרוב
אליך הדבר מאד בפיך ובילבבך לעשתו

*For this commandment which I command you today
is not too discouraging for you, neither is it far. It is
not in Heaven to say who shall go up for us to
Heaven and bring it to us so we can hear it and do
it. And not across the sea is it to say who shall go
across for us, across the sea, and bring it to us so we
may hear it and do it. For very near to you is this
Word, in your mouth and in your heart to do it.*

— *Deuteronomy 30:11-14*

Commentary: Bazak Thirty-nine
בזק"לט אש זרה
The Word — Ha'Devar

A dark Angel at her side, the Soul is on the bank of the River of Descent, about to be born across the waters into the World of Action. It is at this moment that the Angel Mosheh gives her a token that will sustain her in all her days of sojourning across the river, a stranger in a strange land.

Come, listen as the Angel separates this final message from all the urgings and prohibitions, commandments and judgments of the forty years of purification. For all the Torah is holy, but the seven words of this single commandment are most holy, each word an entrance home.

The Angel says the Word is so close to you that no one need bring it to you from Heaven, from the World above you, or from Assiyah, on the other side of the River you are about to cross.

No one has to bring this Word to you. It is not distant because it is always with you. The breath in your mouth and the beating of your heart's blood accompany you each second of your life. In your breath and blood is the Word of God.

כי קרוב אליך הדבר מאד בפיך ובילבבך לעשתו
Ki-karov aleycha ha-davar me'od, beficha uvilvavcha la'a-soto.

The seven words are a talisman to be held as a bright jewel in the mind and a blazing furnace in the heart, a reminder and a promise that in Heaven or Hell, on this or the other side of the Sea of Ending, God is with you and a multitude of angels stand ready to bring you home.

Ki-karov aleycha ha-davar me'od, beficha uvilvavcha la'asoto. For very near to you is the Word, in your mouth and in your heart, to do it.

What are these but the parting words of the parent sending a beloved child off into the world, promising always to be near, urging the child to be faithful.

Consider each word in this final blessing.

כי קרוב *Ki-Karov.* We have met this word, *karov*, in Strange Fire, Bazak Thirty-three , this single phrase that means both "near" and "sacrifice." To come near to YHVH is to make oneself holy by offering one's whole self, to be present and free to practice *devekuth,* attachment in the present, streaming moment.

This is the word the Angel Mosheh whispered to the grief-stricken Aaron to comfort him, and it is embedded in the epitaph to his sons, the holy martyrs Nadav and Abihu. *B'karovay ehkahdaysh,* by those who are near to Me shall I be sanctified.

The willing offering of a life, the burnt offering of a life, rises as the incense of the Lord, as the eternal *Nefesh*, breaks free of its bonds.

אליך *Aleychah*. "To you." In Hebrew this word starts with God (אל, Aleph Lamed) and ends with You (final-Chaf). The simple meaning is identical to the form: God/You. You are being addressed as a single Soul in an ocean of Souls. The Word is part of the Covenant, a granting of largess from YHVH in return for an offering of the flesh. Your flesh.

הדבר *Ha'davar*. *Davar*, meaning "word" or "speech," also means "thing" or "object." Ha'davar is thus "the word" or "the thing" in Hebrew. This relationship between things and words, between body and spirit united in a single sign, might be attributed to the magical properties the Hebrews attached to naming, e.g., Adam and the animals, the Angel and Jacob. The naming of the tribes, of cities and even wells and springs create some intimate bond between the namer and the object, and embody some property in a person or object. The ultimate union of thing and the word is us, the Mud Man, the Spirit in the flesh. In this final blessing, *ha'davar* is taken to mean the Word, but if it were to be translated the Thing, the meaning would be unchanged.

מאד *Me'od*. As an adverb, this word means "very," and modifies *karov*. As a noun, the same word means great and powerful. Here, where only seven words carry the final blessings on the Soul about to born, one is used for emphasis.   *Karov* means to come near, to come close. The Word of YHVH, however, is closer than "*karov*" for in this Word is all your life, it is within you and without. It is *karov me'od.* It is powerfully close.   It is nothing less than Be-ing, the radiant Light on which your life, on which life itself, is suspended, breath by breath, beat by beat.

בפיך B'fichah "in your mouth" ובילבבך uvilvavcha, "and in your heart." The Word is suspended in the breath of your mouth, the beating of your heart. It is this near to each precarious moment of life so the Soul can act, can do it.   What is in the mouth?   In the mouth is the fire-air, the *aysh-ruach* of the human being, the sparkling burning spirit of our lives. And what is in the heart? In the heart is the earth-water, the *adamah-mayim* of our lives pouring its salty torrents throughout our being.   That the mouth and heart are also symbolic of speech and emotion only reinforces the powerful, direct meaning of these words.

To the *nefesh* about to re-enter the flesh — subject to the pain, death, beauty, and distraction of life in the body — the Angel promises that with every breath and with every beat of the heart is the assurance of God's Presence suffusing each instant of being.

לעשתו La'asoto, "to act," is the root of the word Assi-yah, the name of the World to which this Nefesh Chayah, this living soul, is about to descend.   Crafted into this single word is the object of the terrible journey about to begin, again. For to be born, across the Sea of Descent is to act in the world of time. It is only in this bodily form that the *nefesh,* the spiritual soul, can act in the World of Assiyah. From the womb the infant crawls to its pit. To be born into Assiyah is to act, to produce, to do the work of YHVH with the pit as the only certain goal. Between the womb and the pit is the work of our lives, the work of YHVH. And to do it we need not look to others across the sea for orders, nor turn our eyes to heaven, but simply follow the Voice in our breath and heartbeat and just do it. It is our mission. It is our offering.

A Candle in the Night

We are on a journey of shocking inconsistency, a journey illuminated by humor and pathos. It is a human journey, God's journey as a human,

We are spirit encased in a body of earth and water, a concatenation of elements, suffused with the pulse and breath of the Master of the Universe, placed as a candle in the absolute zero night of space, set among flaming seraphim that flare for an instant, then flicker out.

We are set out among the great lights of space, the fiercely burning suns, reflecting crystals of planets and whirling constellations of stars.

We are set in the candlesticks of galaxies, clumps of matter that sag the warp of time.

We are set out to burn. In the web of the Universe we are burning even now.

Sabbath candles are we.

Yahrzeit, memorial, candles are we.

Holy candles in the heart of that great burning.

And yet we suffer and are as buffoons and clowns in the alleys of stars.

The End of Days comes for each of us. Everything that lives flows through the Gates of Death. That which lives, dies. And that which dies, lives.

When the breath of God visits, we arise and live, eat, procreate, dream, sing. When the *ruach ha'Shem* is no longer within our bodies, the tides of *Mayim,* the great Sea tides, ebb and are stilled. Does not the child know this, the dumb animal, the grass of the field?

We leave on that fading breath, riding the *ruach* home in the silent Radiance. The drumbeat that called to us while still in the womb calls to us when we leave the womb of Assiyah. The breath we took when first we crossed the Sea of Descent carries us home.

Ki-karov aleycha ha-davar me'od
For very near to you is the word...

How near is *Karov*? Rabbi Nachman Tiktinner, Ha-Ranit, says *"Karov* is the distance between our breath and our life. *Karov* is the heartbeat of time. "

The *Bahir*

In Rabbi Aryeh Kaplan's translation of the *Bahir*, one of the most ancient kabbalist texts, Rabbi Rahumai says:
> Glory (*Kavod*) and Heart (*Lev*) both have the same [numerical value, namely 32.] They are both one, but Glory refers to its function on high, and Heart refers to its

function below. "God's glory" and the "heart of heaven" are therefore both identical."

We live from breath to breath, from heartbeat to heartbeat, with God's glory in our heart.

What of the Karov of the Absurd?

Glory does not always fill our heart. Come, hear this story. One night, restless and ill, as my wife slept beside me, I lay in bed rehearsing the years, disquieting my soul. My new upper denture irritated. I removed it and, holding it in my hand, fell asleep. When I awoke I was toothless in the dark and could not find the denture.

Heart racing, I checked the bed, and then the bathroom. I walked in the dark to the kitchen to get a flashlight. There, among the cassette tapes, was a flashlight without batteries. I went to the garage, naked and toothless. One plastic flashlight, battered and worn, still worked a little. Returning to the bedroom, I kneeled quietly on the rug in the dark and shined the weak light under the bed.

There on the floor, against the wall, under the dead center of the bed, my teeth smiled reassuringly back at me.

It was the playful grin of conspiracy I saw. *Karov me'od.*

We can be absurd. The same burnt offering set as a candle to the Lord of Creation, burning in the absolute zero of space, can indeed bend over, terrified at not finding a set of false teeth.

And that tidepool heart, pumping the saltwater of this sweet Earth, was it not fibrillating that night in fear and vanity?

And, the holy *ruach*, was it not squeezed and constrained by the shallow rise and fall of terrified calculation?

We live from breath to breath, from heartbeat to heartbeat.

> *The word is very near. In your mouth And*
> *in your heart. That you may do it.*

We may do it. And we may not. In our hurly burly life we are holy candle and fool. We can choose to stop and hear the Word in our mouth and heart.

Sometimes the *nefesh* soars to the singing light of creation, sometimes we grope, naked, for a plastic flashlight to search for our false teeth. Welcome to the human condition, colorfully characterized in Yiddish as *ferblundgeta fartz*, lost farts in a blizzard, candles in the winds of change, living *karov me'od* to the source of all Being.

To What Are We Born?

Simply crossing the Sea of Descent requires innocence and a leap of faith.

We are born blind and deaf, a slave to our appetites from the very beginning. From the womb to the pit we are accompanied by the reassuring lub-dub of the Eternal

128

Mother's heartbeat. Our first breath, the sparkling *ruach* awaits us as we arrive, all wet and bloody, howling and shaking across the Sea of Descent. Welcome to Assiyah.

We may marvel at the miracles of form yet know they will betray us. Our arm, cunning in its capillaries and neurons, muscled and reliable, will lose its power, shrivel. And yet it is still our arm, ours alone, the arm that shields our child, cradles our guitar. Holds our beloved.

In this dual, schizophrenic world, where flesh and spirit come together to make us, to form us, can we even approach the Master of the Universe — to say, as Abraham says, "Behold now I have taken it on myself to talk to God, I who am but dust and ashes " — to ask why and to what end?

It is an end that is not given us to see, but we may know, directly, *the Word is very near, in your mouth and in your heart to do it.*

The Covenant of New Life

YHVH, the Eternal Lord of all the universe, the Creator, covenants before we cross the waters, to wash us in the *ruach,* the spirit of God, in each breath. And in each heartbeat, in the tides of blood washing all our body of mud, if we are still, we can hear the echoes of our home, as the sea can be heard in a conch.

It is a Covenant that has never been broken with any living organism. We are continually supported, constantly reminded that we come from some other place, for our breath does not originate with us, nor did we create our heartbeat.

And yet we must take this new body, this body that will be born wet and blind across the Sea, and suffer the pains and joys of living under the light of an earthly sun, and with bones that break, and muscles that tear, rise up to hear this Voice that whispers in our veins, hear this Voice that calls us home, and attach ourselves to YHVH that we may be holy.

That attachment, *devekuth*, calls us to detach from self, from home and children, detach far enough to enter the present, streaming, unfolding moment. To Be. In our heart is the glory of God. To choose to be in that glory is to choose life itself.

Bazak Forty
בזק"מ   ובחרת בחיים
Vacharta Ba'chayim — Choose Life

העדתי בכם היום את־השמים ואת־הארץ החיים
והמות נתתי לפניך הברכה והקללה ובחרת בחיים
למען תחיה אתה וזרעך לאהבה
את־יהוה אלהיך לשמע בקלו ולדבקה־בו כי הוא
חייך וארך ימיך לשבת על־האדמה אשר נשבע
יהוה לאבתיך לאברהם ליצחק וליעקב לתת להם

*I call heaven and earth as witness against you today,
life and death I place before you, the blessing and
the curse. Choose life so you may live, you and your
children, to love YHVH your God, to hear His
voice and to cleave to Him, for He is your life and
the light of your days as you dwell on the land which
YHVH swore to your fathers, to Abraham, to Isaac,
and to Jacob, to give to them.*

— Deuteronomy 30:19,20

Commentary: Bazak Forty
בזק"מ ובחרת בחיים
Vacharta Ba'chayim — Choose Life

Asaph stands on the banks of the water. From here the River of Descent does not seem very wide. It is easy to see across the dark, slow moving water to the date palms, the olive trees and low hills on the other side. Around him there is much activity as the priests ready the Ark of the Word for the journey across and the tribes organize for their crossing to the Promised Land.

It has been said the waters will part when the priests' feet enter the river. And the virgin earth will open for their passage, just as it did when they first entered the Wilderness through the Sea of Ending.

Across the River, in the World of Assiyah, are those the turrets of Gilgal gleaming in the bright Sun or just the glinting of light in the distance?

Asaph feels the rising excitement. He has grown content here, the slow passage of these desert days, the service of the Tabernacle, the sweet air. But in the deep stirring around him, he senses all is ready and soon he will be moving across. He hears the voice of the Angel Mosheh rise behind him. " *Choose life so you may live, you and your children, to love YHVH your God, to hear His voice and to cleave to Him, for He is your life and the light of your days.* "

Here, near the end of *The Hebrew Book of the Dead,* a story extending from the creation of the world to the birth, death, and resurrection of Asaph, a Living Soul, the Angel Mosheh is about to make his own *aliyah.* It is his birthday — "I am a hundred and twenty years old this day" — and in this self same day will he move on to his next life. He shall not go across the Jordan, the Sea of Descent, because he is not to be reborn in Assiyah. His home is not among the world of humans across the Sea of Descent. He is commanded to "go up to the mountain and die...and be carried off to your people." On his birthday, Moses will be carried off. (The Hebrew root for "carried off" is *asaph.*) And he now distances himself from the children of Israel, prefacing his final oration, "What does the Lord require of *you...?*"

It is also Asaph's birthday, for this day will he leave Yetzirah to cross the Jordan and descend into time and flesh in the World of Assiyah. It is time to be born.

In Bazak Forty, the *nefesh chayah,* the living soul, hears the final instructions of the Angel Mosheh. About to descend into garments of flesh and bone and blood, Asaph is urged to prepare himself for the crossing, to choose life, choose the blessing.

It is not by choice that Asaph enters the World of Action, the world of decay and time. But once born, once on this Earth, he must continually choose between life and death, between the blessings and the curse.

In the Mishnah tractate, *Pirkey Aboth*, Rabbi Elazar HaKappar says:

> *Those who are born will die; those who are*
> *dead will be revived....Know that everything is*
> *according to the reckoning and let not your*
> *imagination give you hope that the grave will be*
> *a place of refuge for you. For against your will*
> *were you formed, and against your will were*
> *you born, and against your will do you live, and*
> *against your will do you die....*

The Witness, the *Gematriya*

What is this "witness" called by the Angel Mosheh? What is this word and how can we tear away its covering to get at its heart? From what place, with what force, against which organs, cords, tongue, teeth, palate, cheek and lips has it come to carry its message?

One way to understand a word is to take it apart and put its parts alongside each other. In Hebrew, it is the consonants that do all the serious work, the vowels simply carrying, joining and modifying their congregation. And each of those twenty-two consonants is a nation with followers, with pretensions and ancestors beyond the Arameans and Phoenicians, already ancient in the time of the pharaohs.

A chief characteristic of *The Hebrew Book of the Dead* is that it was written in Hebrew. Beyond the coded history in each sound, every letter represents a number, every word a combination of numbers. From this did the kabbalists derive the machinery of the *sephirot*, from this did David number his legions. *Gematriya* is the system through which meaning is derived from words by means of the numerical value of the consonants. It is a very ancient practice, already use in the time of Assyrian king Sargon, in the Eighth Century B.C.E.

Beyond numbers, the names of Hebrew letters refer to objects as well. The Hebrew ב, "bayt," the second letter in the alphabet, is also the symbol for the number 2 and means "house." Combining letter symbolism and numeric equivalencies is one way to shut out distractions and develop the deep *kavannah,* concentration, that can yield spiritual insights leading to attachment to God.

Although it may be disconcerting to the reader whose native language is not Hebrew, standing the letters against the wall this way, measuring their height and weight, comparing them with each other, back to back, is as good a way of deriving hidden meaning as listening to them bang around each other in a whistling, sucking, plosive chorus punctuated by shrugged shoulders and wry eyebrows.

Gematriya provides a glimpse of another World wheeling just beneath or around our own commonplace reality. It is a World of numbers that offer hints and allusions of secret meanings. Like dreams, these numbers can be significant or amusing. Sometimes they can be illuminating.

A popular *gematriya,* for example, applied to the Tetragrammaton, YHVH, yields the number 26. י, Yod, the tenth letter in the Hebrew alphabet, is the symbol for the number 10. ה, Hay, the fifth letter, the number 5 and ו, Vav, the sixth letter, number 6. YHVH is thus 26.

Using the same system, the Hebrew word for one, *echod,* yields the number 13, as does the Hebrew word for love, *ahavah.* Thus there is a relationship drawn between God, on the one hand, and love and oneness on the other. Echod + Ahavah = 26. YHVH=26.

Consider the *gematriya* for העדתי, *ha'idoti,* the first word in the text:

העדתי בכם היום
Ha'idoti vachem hayom,
I witness against you this day.

Ha'idoti is a composite Hebrew form and at its heart is Ayd (עד). Ayin ע and Dalet ד. Ayin-Dalet. Together it means a door that opens and and an eye that sees.

Ayin means "eye," and is also the number 70. Dalet in Hebrew means "door," and is also the number four.

Ayin, the eye (70) and Dalet the door (4). Together they are 74. The Eye that sees and the Door through which you walk. Ayin-Dalet. Together they make a Witness because 74 = 7+4 = 11. The number 11 is made up of 1+1. I and Thou. The Witness and you. The Eye that sees, the door through which you walk. You are given a choice and there is One who sees that you were given the choice of life or death.

In the Ninth Commandment, Thou shalt not bear false witness, you will find an *Ayd.* Ayin-Dalet.

But there is another use of the same Ayin-Dalet. It can be found in the Psalms: "and the Lord shall live forever and ever." Forever, everlasting. *L'olam v'ayd.* It is used this way in the Book of the Chronicles of the Kings, in the time of Daniel, and to this very day. Ayin-Dalet is forever. 74.

It is a witness for all Eternity, a witness forever that you were offered the choice of the Blessing of Life and the Curse of Death.

Who Would Choose Death?

You will be born, carried across the River on the shoulders of Priests. In this you have no choice. You are simply doing the work of the Lord. Remember this day, says the Angel Mosheh, that you may know you do have a choice in the World across the River, a choice between life and death. Chose life that you may be free in the World of Assiyah.

And yet, in the stiffness of our necks and the arrogance of our hearts, do we not often choose death, the death of a thousand masks and costumes? The worship of material wealth is so rampant that the world has been given over to commerce, fanning the greed and envy of its myriads of souls.

But where are the priests for peace and love, for the continual quiet holiness of life? We are not awed but distracted by our entertainments, our holy moments on Earth stolen in the flickering blue light of a TV tube, our games. We choose death in a thousand ways.

When we turn away from suffering and close our hearts, lock our doors against the poor and weak, when we swell with pride and when we fear, have we not chosen yet another death?

Against the blessing of a life in God is the curse of death, living so that God is hidden from us. We are separated from our Soul when we no longer feel YHVH's Presence or hear YHVH's voice as we crawl along, blind and deaf, in the tumultuous World of Assiyah.

The Way of *Devekuth*

Choose life so you may live, you and your children, to love YHVH your God, to hear His voice and to cleave to Him

Come, listen. These words have been before our eyes and ears for more than three millennia. Read not, "Choose life so that you and your children may live;" but read the actual ancient text: "Choose life so that you and your children may live *to love God your Lord.* "

Le'ahavah et-YHVH, love YHVH, are the words of the Hebrew Scripture. Here in Assiyah, and in all our days in all of God's Worlds, YHVH is our life.

The blessing of life is to be on this Earth, loving God. How is it possible to love God?

There are many paths in *The Hebrew Book of the Dead,* but *devekuth*, attachment to God, is the object of each path. To undertake that journey, the Soul must be *chofesh,* free, for the path toward *devekuth* is not open to slaves. Whether in the Wilderness with the children of Israel, or in the grip of the loves and ambitions of Assiyah, until the *nefesh* is free, *devekuth* is unattainable.

To embrace *devekuth* is to become free of the dark winter of exile, to renew the springtime of the loving Covenant between each of us and God:

For, lo, the winter is past,
The rain is over and gone.
The flowers appear on the earth,
The time of singing is come,
And the voice of the turtle is heard in our land.
The fig-tree puts forth her green figs
And the vines in blossom give forth their fragrance,
Arise, my love, my fair one, and come away.

Hear Gershom Scholem on this:

> The kabbalists unanimously agreed on the supreme rank attainable by the soul at the end of its mystical path, namely, that of devekuth, mystical cleaving to God. In turn, there might be different ranks of devekuth itself, such as "(equanimity," *hishtavvut,* the indifference of the soul to praise or blame), "solitude" *(hitbodedut,* being alone with God).

Such is the ladder of *devekuth.* Choose to be free that you may hear, love and attach yourself —*devkah-bo* —to God.

There is an outcome to all our choices. Rabbi Abraham Abulafia says,

Whoever is drawn toward the vanities of temporality, his soul shall survive in the vanities of temporality and whoever is drawn after the Name... which is above temporality, his soul shall survive in the eternal realm beyond time, in God, may He be blessed.

Without *devekuth* there is essential loneliness, the emptiness felt in a loveless, silent, separated world. To choose a life without *devekuth* is to choose death. It is what we do when we choose the Tree of Knowledge and by-pass the Tree of Life.

The Cleft in the Rock

The love of the Angel Mosheh for YHVH, the Way of *Devekuth*, led him to the *nikrat tzur*, to the Cleft of the Rock. It is a place of great power and holiness, available to each of us, at all times, in this life.

> "Lord, says the Angel Mosheh,, if I have found favor in your eyes let me see Your glory. "
> "You cannot see My face and live, but I will hide you in the Cleft of the Rock and you may see My back when I pass."
> — from *Exodus 33:12-23*

For those who urgently, desperately, seek God, the *nikrat tzur* is a holy site, to be cherished and tended, with whole meditations devoted to the rocky ascent leading to

141

this sanctuary. It as if God has said, "There is this secret place within, where My face coming toward you, the future arriving, the cauldron of Creation, cannot be seen, but I will shield you with My hand as I pass. In the stitch of my passing Glory as I leave you, the departing present moment can be glimpsed. "

The cleft in the rock is *karov me'od,* as close as we can get in this World to the present streaming moment. In that moment only can we say, *hinani,* behold, I am here. And that moment is all the time we have. It is life itself. Not in regret for the past nor hope for the future is our life, but only now, in this intersection of time, do we live. Only in this present streaming moment can we be.

My Face and My back.

You cannot see My *panai*, My face. *Panai* means both face or forepart and the state of anticipation, the future. Before something takes place is *al panai.* You cannot see the approaching future as it is being created, but you may see My back, *acharai,* which means both "back" and "afterward." You may see my Glory departing.

Is this not just a fundamental reality of the physical universe?

Even fully aware, our perception of the present is delayed by the reflection of light to our receptors, the concussion of sound across air and eardrum, the crackling of our neural pathways. Our physical body prohibits immediacy. From the Cleft in the Rock we may approach closer to the present streaming moment, the Word. We may come *karov me'od,* very near, to the source of Creation. In that approach we feel our whole being losing its false sense of Self in anticipation of coming near the Beloved.

It is the outcome of perfect *devekuth.*

In the electric intersection of the approaching future and departing past, in that narrow space between two eternities, we may truly choose life, simply by being in the present moment, God's moment, the only moment briefly given to us in Assiyah.

As the prophet Isaiah wrote:

> To go into the clefts of the rocks and into the
> crevices of the crags, from before the terror of
> the Lord and from the glory of His majesty.

In the narrow cleft in which we live, between life and life, the way is hard and dark, for we are born blind and stumble through our days, now exultant, now tremulous, starting at sounds in the dark, swelling at the approval of the blind hordes among whom we live.

There is another way. It is the Way of Holiness.

The Way of Holiness

In the Way of Holiness all paths are open and flooded with light. As Isaiah prophesied:

> And a highway shall be there and a way

The unclean and the fool shall not pass over
It shall be called the Way of Holiness.

This is the path that continues from the desert wilderness, the Midbar, across the Jordan, the Sea of Descent, to our birth, to choose life. It is the path of holiness. To choose requires freedom to choose.

Is this not told in the story of the Hebrew slave? "You shall be holy, for I your Lord am holy." The requirement to be free is the requirement to have no master of your Soul for how can God have a master?

To take a master is to bow to a golden calf, to renew the slavery of our early days in the Wilderness, and the slavery that calls us now in this World of Assiyah. After that dance around the golden calf, YHVH hid himself from the children of Israel as God is hidden from us to this day. In the closed heart we no longer feel God's Presence in our bodies. Our vision grows flat and cynical. We worship created things.

Aysh Zarah — The Sacrifice

It took a willing sacrifice, the death of Nadav and Abihu, to redeem the soul of Asaph (see Bazak Thirty-three, Strange Fire). The sons of the high priest offered themselves as a fire offering to free their father and the community of Israel, to atone for the sin of the golden calf. It is a holy act that takes place in our own Souls, in our own time.

It took a willing sacrifice, a burnt offering, to bring Asaph across the Jordan River to the city of Gilgal, the Resurrection City by the Sea. That burning cleared the soul of Asaph from slavery and redeemed the chosen son of Israel.

To choose life is to choose to be in the Cleft in the Rock.

To choose to be free, to be nothing, is to choose life itself. We cannot live on the mountain and do our work in this World. But through the practice of *devekuth* we can find a path to God in our days. In this way do we draw *me'od*, very near, to holiness. To be in the present moment in the World of Action is to embrace the holiness in this world.

God so loves us that we are held in this life in continual contact with the Substance of all Being, in our very veins and lungs, in the lumens of our bodies. We are never abandoned.

For He is your life and the light of your days when you dwell on the Earth.

Adamah, the word that means earth, the word from which Adam, the primordial man was created, is made up of *Aleph* and *Dam*. *Aleph* is One, the life force, the first flaming letter, the letter of *Emet,* truth. *Dam* is Hebrew for blood. We dwell with the Source of life within our blood, for we are *A-dam*.

And when we step out of this garment of flesh, and the last sparkling *Ruach* is released, and when our body is returned to the mud from which it was made, we will have ended this span in the World of Action. Did we love God and do mercy and justice in His name? Did we struggle to be in his shining, present, streaming moment?

Before we are stripped of this garment of flesh, minute by minute in our days in Assiyah, we choose the blessing of life or the curse. We can choose life in our very last moment. We can choose life right now.

Summary: Bazak Forty-one

As Joshua prepares to take over leadership of the quest from Moses, he reminds the children of Israel how God kept the covenant from Egypt through the desert. In Bazak Forty-One, at the banks of the Jordan, with the city of Gilgal in sight, he cautions the Israelites to watch the ark of the covenant, the ark that holds the bones of Asaph and the Word of God, so "you may know the way by which you must go. For you have not passed this way before." And when they see the priests bearing the ark move forward, they follow at a distance. The waters of the Jordan are about to part.

The Hebrew Book of the Dead

148

Bazak Forty-Two
בזק מ"ב הברית
The Covenant - Ha'Brit

הנה ארון הברית אדון כל־הארץ עבר
לפניכם בירדן ויעמדו הכהנים נ'שאי
הארון ברית־יהוה בחרבה בתוך הירדן
הכן וכל־ישראל עברים בחרבה עד
אשר־תמו כל־הגוי לעבור את־הירדן
והעם עלו מן־הירדן בעשור לחדש הראשון
ויחנו בגלגל בקצה מזרח יריחו

*Behold, the Ark of the Covenant of the Lord of all
the Earth passes over before you across the Jordan.
And the priests that carried the covenant of YHVH
stood on dry ground in the midst of the Jordan until
all Israel passed over on dry ground, until all the nation was passed completely over the Jordan. And the
people came up out of the Jordan on the tenth day of
the first month and camped in Gilgal to the extreme
east of Jericho.*

—*Joshua 3:11,17. 4:19*

Commentary: Bazak Forty-two
בזק"מב הברית
Ha'Brit - The Covenant

It is spring, the month of Aviv, the first month of the
year, and a time to be born. In Assiyah, the first green
buds appear as the winter's dark chill recedes. A
mother, nearing the end of her long pregnancy, sits by the
window and breathes the perfumed air.

Her fetus, swimming in a saline sea, listens to his
mother's heart. In all his long becoming there has been no
weather, no heat, no chilling wind, no life outside this
aron-rechem, this womb-ark, as he becomes incarnate. Instant by instant, he becomes *ad-tohm*, becomes whole. Instant by instant, the embryo in the womb is consumed by
the man-child about to be born.

The walls of the womb-ark contract and open, burst-
ing the waters that lie between his dark world and the
bright, clanging, sparkling world to come. Beyond, a dark
stranger watches as the infant bursts into this world and
draws his first breath on Earth.

He is dried and cleaned and wrapped in a swaddling
blanket. He is given water and put to his mother's breast.
He breathes the air and eats the food of the Earth.

It is spring. Arise, come up out of the Waters of Descent.

Joshua prepared the children of Israel for their passage.
"When you see the Ark of the Covenant of YHVH your

151

God, and the priests the Levites bearing it, then shall you remove from your place and go after it so you may know the way by which you must go. For you have not passed this way before. "

Now it is time. "Behold the Ark of the Covenant of the Lord of all the earth passes over before you across the Jordan."

The flesh shall follow the Word. You have known no weather, no struggle for food, no life outside this *midbar,* this desert wilderness. You have followed the Ark from Sinai to the Waters of Descent leading to this Promised Land. It is time to be born.

Across the waters they come, on the dry land, between the flooding Waters of Descent they come, the children of Israel, streaming past the priests carrying the Ark of the Covenant, standing on dry land in the midst of the Jordan, streaming past carrying the bones of Asaph, in the Ark, across to the Promised Land.

They come up on the tenth day of the first month. *And the people came up from the Waters of Descent.* Rising up to be reborn. Four days before Passover, the day the children of Israel left Egypt forty years earlier, they rise up to be reborn in the Promised Land.

The Covenant in the Flesh

The first act of the children of Israel in the World of Assiyah is to affirm the Covenant of Blood.

It is for the sake of that Covenant that the bones of Asaph have come across the Midbar to Canaan, for this is

152

the land promised to his fathers by YHVH. For YHVH told Jacob, "I will protect you wherever you go and will bring you back to this land. I will not leave you until I have done what I have promised you." Asaph, the chosen son of Israel, has been brought back to fulfil the Covenant. His bones will be buried in the Promised Land.

The wandering children of Israel have come up, out of the Sea of Descent, out of the Jordan, and are born into the material world. The Ark of the Covenant that has come up from the Jordan on the shoulders of the priests contains the Word. Now the Covenant must be written in the flesh, in the flesh of a new body.

The Covenant, or *brit,* emerges from the mists of the earliest days, the agreement between God and the Patriarch that set this people on its path. When Abraham was ninety-nine years old, YHVH appeared to him and said,

> I am God, El Shaddai. Walk before Me and be pure. I will make My Covenant with you and you will be exceedingly numerous. I will make you fruitful and I will make nations of you and kings shall come out of you. I will give you and your seed all the land of Canaan for an everlasting possession.
>
> And as for you, you shall keep My Covenant you and your seed after you throughout their generations. This is My Covenant which you shall keep between Me and you and your seed after you. Every male among you shall be circumcised.
>
> — *Genesis 17:1-11*

153

Circumcise Again, the Second Time

It is the first act in the Promised Land. YHVH said to Joshua:

> Make you knives of flint and circumcise the children of Israel the second time. And circumcise again the children of Israel the second time. So Joshua had flint knives made and the children of Israel were circumcized.

Why were the children of Israel circumcised a second time? The Covenant with Abraham is unequivocal: *And you shall circumcise the flesh of your foreskin, and it shall be a sign of the Covenant between Me and you.* The men who rose up out of the Jordan into flesh had been circumcised and enslaved in Egypt. Now they were free and whole, renewed in spirit and newly risen into the flesh.

> For the children of Israel walked forty years in the wilderness till all the nation, even the men of war that came forth out of Egypt, were completed (*ad-tohm*).

The men of war were not killed in the Wilderness nor did they die. They were *ad-tohm*, completed, from the Hebrew *tamam*, where *ad-tohm* means complete, to be made whole. For example: "They abode in their places in camp till they were whole *(ad- hayotahm).* "

The Ancient Hebrews did not think the men of war were killed in the wilderness, for did not Moses address them on the banks of the Jordan in the eleventh month of the fortieth year in the *Midbar* and say:

> He gave you manna to eat that you knew not, neither did your fathers know, that he might make you know that man does not live by bread only, but by whatever the mouth of God brings forth does man live.

These words, spoken on the eve of the great entry to the Promised Land, are spoken to those who knew the food of Egypt. They are the ones who *knew not manna.* They who had been circumcised in Egypt would now, re-born in the Holy Land, be circumcised again.

And why were the new born Israelites not circumcised in the Midbar?

There were no conceptions or births in the Midbar. There were no circumcisions in the Desert Wilderness of Yetzirah because the *brit milah*, the covenant of circumcision, is a covenant of blood in the flesh, and the wanderers in the *midbar* had neither blood nor flesh but were travelers in the wilderness between two Worlds, Souls in the process of becoming *ad-tohm*, whole, so they might cross the Waters of Descent and be born in the Promised Land.

And why were the children of Israel circumcised again on their first day in the Promised Land?

The advent of the full moon of Aviv and Passover is to appear four days after the children of Israel rose out of the Sea of Descent to be reborn in the Promised Land. No uncircumcised male may celebrate the Passover with the children of Israel.

Passover and the End of the Manna

> And the children of Israel camped at Gilgal, and they made the passover on the fourteenth day of the month toward evening in the plains of Jericho.

The first camp of the children of Israel in the Promised Land is Gilgal, the Wheel. It is the kabbalist word for reincarnation. It is here that the Israelites become fully human.

> And they did eat of the produce of the land on the morning after Passover, unleavened cakes and parched corn, in the selfsame day, And the manna ceased on the morrow, after they had eaten of the produce of the land; neither had the children of Israel manna any more; but they did eat of the fruit of the land of Canaan that year.

The *Zohar* says:

The food found by Israel that time in the desert, (comes) from the higher sphere called Heaven --it is an even finer food, entering deepest of all into the soul, detached from the body, called "angel bread."

Daniel Matt illuminates this text in the notes to his translation of the *Zohar:* "Ordinary food grows from the ground and is fed by rain but manna derives from Heaven (*Tiferet*). This food bypasses the body and nourishes the soul."

The Prince of Hosts

The rites of passage have been observed. The bones of Joseph are brought safely into the Promised Land, and the circumcision of the newborn soul has ratified the Covenant of the Land. The Passover matzah, the meal that ended slavery in Egypt, is eaten again, this time in freedom in the Promised Land.

Manna no longer suckles the soul, and the *Nefesh Chayah* eats the food of the holy land. All that had been put into motion when Moses first stood by the Burning Bush has now been completed. That this great journey across the desert to rebirth is now complete, that this is indeed the holy land, is announced by the Dark Angel.

And it came to pass when Joshua was by Jericho that he lifted up his eyes and looked, and behold, there stood a man over against him with his sword drawn in his hand, and Joshua went unto him and said unto him, "Are you

157

for us or for our adversaries?" And he said,
"No, but I am Prince of the host of the Lord.
I am now come." And the Prince of the
Lord's host said to Joshua, "Put off your shoe
from your foot for the place whereon you
stand is holy.

Are We Not, Today, on Holy Ground?

In our lives today, as then — born and covenanted,
depending on food that grows from the ground, en-
chanted by possibilities and beset by dark forces, in our
life in this body of flesh, before us in all our days —
stands the dark angel, sword in hand.

He is neither for us nor for our adversaries. He is the
Prince of the Lord of Hosts who has come before us into
this Promised Land to enforce the covenant. Our blessing
is to cleave to YHVH, and our curse is to be cast off into
the illusions of this world and into the hands of men.

Thus does *The Hebrew Book of the Dead* draw to an
end.

Let us not be as a Watcher in the Night, for it is our
own life that is filled with blessings and curses. Our youth
ends in a Pit in the Wilderness, for we are the Dreamer
who is sold into the slavery of Assiyah.

We were raised up to power and we will soon be
placed in a Pit in the Lower Kingdom and brought up to
the Gates of the Sea of Ending. All life in God is em-
barked in the explosive Creation speeding infinitely away

from the infinitely radiating center of Be-ing. This is our home, our true and only home. And the Covenant extends over all.

Martin Buber wrote:

> Men do not find God if they stay in the world. They do not find Him if they leave the world. He who goes out with all his being to meet his Thou and carries to it all being that is in the world, finds Him who cannot be sought.

God's Love?

With our soul and with our senses we can feel God's love, feel the movement, the continual gentle presence of the spirit in our flesh. We can feel the flash of recognition, hear the rapture of music, see the rising light reflecting in cascades of brilliance around us. We know God's love with our senses, the neurons of our soul's life in Assiyah, plugged into the fiery, saline heart of Assiyah with the pods of our senses, feeding and fighting in the briny heart of this World of Fire. Nefesh Chayot are we. Living Beings are we, souls in the flesh, children of the Lord of all the Universe.

Ahead is our life with its Blessings and its Curses, and beyond that there is the Midbar. Over it all, over all the Worlds is the Covenant of God's enduring love.

Summary: Bazak Forty-three

Once the children of Israel have entered the Promised Land they have left the World of Yetzirah. They are no longer among the angels. They are in this World of Assiyah and are once again flesh and the Covenant that brought them across the Wilderness must be ratified in the flesh. Joshua is ordered to "Circumcise again, the second time, the children of Israel." They celebrate the Passover on the fourteenth day. The manna ceases after the children of Israel had eaten of the produce of the Land. After the foundation wars, the children of Israel are ready for the final act of *The Hebrew Book of the Dead*.

Bazak Forty-Four
בזק מ"ד בחלקת השדה
In an Open Field - B'chelkaht ha'sadeh

ואת־עצמות יוסף אשר־העלו בני־ישראל
ממצרים קברו בשכם בחלקת השדה אשר
קנה יעקב מאת בני־חמור אבי־שכם במאה
קשיטח ויהיו לבני־יוסף לנחלה

*And the bones of Asaph, which the children of Israel
brought up out of Egypt, they buried in Shechem in
the open field that Jacob bought from the sons of
Hamor, the father of Shechem, for a hundred kissi-
tim, and it became, to the children of Asaph, a
possession.*

— Joshua 24:32

161

The Hebrew Book of the Dead

Commentary: Bazak Forty-Four
בחלקת השדה
B'chelkaht ha'sadeh -- In an Open Field

The Rabbis tell this legend:

> The Exodus would have been impossible if Joseph's bones had remained behind. Therefore Moses made it his concern to seek their resting-place.... As soon as he came near them he knew them to be what he was seeking, by the fragrance they exhaled and spread around. But his difficulties were not at an end. The question arose how he was to secure possession of the remains. Joseph's coffin had been sunk far down into the ground, and he knew not how to raise it from the depths. Standing at the edge of the grave, he spoke these words, "Joseph, the time hath come whereof thou didst say, 'God will surely visit you, and you shall carry up my bones from hence.'" No sooner had this reminder dropped from his lips than the coffin stirred and rose to the surface."
>
> —Louis Ginzberg, *Legends of the Bible*

The Exodus itself would have been impossible without this action because the journey across the Midbar, the Desert Wilderness, is the journey of Asaph's bones into the Promised Land, fulfilling the Covenant of YHVH. It is this Ark that will soon be joined by the Ark of acacia wood that will hold the Testimony and the Covenant. Together they cross the Waters of Descent and are brought up to the Promised Land. These are the words of the Torah.

When Moses was tending his father-in-law's flocks in Horeb, an Angel of the Lord appeared to him in a flame of fire out of the midst of a thornbush. The Voice of God sent him out to free the children of Israel from the bondage of Pharaoh. This feat required Moses to take up the bones of Asaph and bring them across the Midbar to the Promised Land. In this final bazak of *The Hebrew Book of the Dead,* the children of Israel complete the transition from the Midbar, and the spiritual World of Yetzirah, to the material world of Assiyah.   The bones of Asaph, brought across the World of Yetzirah at so great a price, are buried in Shechem in the Promised Land.

Shechem is the place where Abraham first came when he entered into the Covenant and left Haran for the Promised Land. Shechem is where Jacob pitched his tent and bought land when he returned to Canaan after his long exile. It is the place to which Asaph headed to find his brothers pasturing their flocks, the beginning of his life's journey. And at the end, it is the place where these generations of the Covenant have come full circle. For it is here that the Covenant is fulfilled.

Returning the bones to this field is to plant them in the earth in fulfillment of the Covenant for now the children of Israel have been brought back to the land, as

YHVH promised. The bones of Asaph, the Tree of Death (see Bazak Seventeen), are returned to the Land, ultimately to rise up again, cycling through the holy Worlds of YHVH.

The commercial details of this mystical transaction — the history of the contract and deed, the accounting of the money paid and the rights to the property in perpetuity — conclude the verse that tells of the burial of Asaph. The mundane issues of possession and money thus confirm the arrival of the Israelites in the flesh and blood world of Canaan.

The bones of Asaph are buried in an open field in the *adamah* that is holy. That these bones will rise again, watered by the sweet dew of heaven, is a belief widely held by the Ancient Hebrews.

In the words of the prophet Isaiah:

יחיו מתיך הקיצו ורננו שכני עפר
כי טל אורת טלך

*Yichyu meteikhah ha'kitzu v'rannu shochnay afar
ki tal orot tahleykha*

*Your dead shall live.
Awake and sing, sleepers in the dust, for a dew of light
is your dew.*

—*Isaiah: 26:19*

Appendix A
The Hebrew Book of the Dead —
Reflections of a Conservative Rabbi

From *the Zohar:*

As R. Judah was once walking along with R. Abba, he said to him: 'I should like to ask you one question. Seeing that God knew that man was destined to sin and to be condemned to death, why did He create him? That He knew this is proved by the fact that in the Torah, which existed two thousand years before the universe, we find it already written, "When a man shall die..." and so forth. Why does God want man in this world, seeing that if he studies the Torah he dies, and if he does not study he also dies, all going one way.' He replied: 'What business have you with the ways and the decrees of your Master? What you are permitted to know and to inquire into, that you may ask, and as for what you are not permitted to know, it is written: "Suffer not thy mouth to cause thy flesh to sin.".' He said to him: 'If that is the case, all the Torah is secret and recondite, since it is the Holy Name, and if so we have no permission to ask and inquire?' He replied: 'The Torah is both hidden and revealed, and the Holy Name is also hidden and revealed, as it is writ-

> ten, "The hidden things belong to the
> Lord our God, and the revealed things
> are for us and for our children."

What are we doing here in this world if, in the end,
we will all die? This is the question we all come
to, and it is the motivation for much of our spiritual life.
What is the meaning of our lives? What are we to do
with our days on Earth? How shall we know if what we
have done with our lives has been valuable, meaningful,
good, and right?

It would be helpful if the answers to these questions
were straightforward, if we knew the answers at birth and
had only to follow those instructions to then die fulfilled,
or to choose to do otherwise and accept the consequences.
But, as our teachers in the Zohar relate, that information
is not easily to be found. Some of it is revealed, and some
of it is hidden. In the end, we seek instruction, we seek
teaching, we seek a path to wholeness. That quest has one
of three goals: to escape death, to embrace death, or to
manage to live life despite its seeming futility in the face
of death.

One of the great teachings pointing the way along one
of those paths is the Hebrew Bible, and particularly its
first section, the Torah, the Five Books of Moses. This
path will be difficult, demanding. Rather than offer a
means to transcend death, and rather than celebrating a
cult of death, the Torah offers one way to live in the face
of death: to accept God's sovereignty and to enter into
covenant with God. The terms of that covenant will be
the commandments of the Torah. Although no individual
will have the opportunity to observe them all, and in the

end, no one will observe even those they can fully or without mistake, the way toward life is to serve God by striving to keep the commandments. In each act one is brought over and over into relationship with God through the enactment of the covenant. Life is neither embraced nor denied but found in the daily individual and collective embrace of the covenant and the commandments.

The instruction offered in the Torah is both hidden and revealed — presented in narrative, directed in statute, hinted at in the very structure of the world described by it. One classical homiletic points to the very first verse as it appears in the King James translation, "In the Beginning, God" and stops there. That is what we need to know first, and perhaps even last. Whatever our personal question might be about how we should live our lives, about the point of our lives, it can only be answered in light of God's Presence and Primacy. As the narrative proceeds, it becomes clear that this world was made for us human beings – that we might live and procreate and enjoy its benefits. We are not God, but we live in God's world. We are God's guests, tenants, and all that we will need to know is how to behave properly in that regard. A guide that might help us manage to live well during all the days that we might abide on this earth is found in the various legal codes and passages throughout the text.

One aspect of that guidance refers us back to the first verse of Genesis. When God brings the Israelites out of Egypt to Sinai, there to receive the laws of the covenant, it is so that they should acknowledge that "I am the Lord your God." That fact, that truth of Creation, leads to covenant and relationship. "You have seen what I did to the Egyptians, how I bore you on eagles' wings and brought you to Me. Now then, if you obey Me faithfully and keep my covenant, you shall be My treasured possession among all the peoples." The benefit of that relationship, the consequence of following the laws of the covenant, is expressed in, "You shall keep My laws and My rules, by pursuit of which man shall live: I am the Lord." So urgent was the desire that the people find life through the pursuit of the covenant that in the Torah Moses says, "I call Heaven and Earth to witness against you this day: I have put before you life and death, blessing and curse. Choose life — if you and your offspring would live."

"Choose life!" – the byword of the Torah. Death is not denied, and death is not embraced. It is present, unavoidable, but not the only option so long as one is yet alive. The promise, clearly, is not that death will not come. Rather, it is through the choice to live, to follow the path of the covenant, that whatever is given will be full, whole, and blessed.

In the course of the liturgical year the Torah is read in full in the synagogue. A section is read each week on the Sabbath, in sequence, from beginning to end. In the concluding moment, we read, "So Moses the servant of the Lord died there . . . before all Israel" and then immediately return to the first verse, "In the beginning, God." For weeks upon end, from the first mention of the infant Moses in Exodus 2:1 through to the very last verse of the Torah, Moses has held center stage. He has been the leader, he has been the prophet, he has been the face of God before the people. The whole of the endeavor of the Exodus and the passage to the Promised Land has been at his direction, in his presence. And then he is gone. In the end, it is only God Who remains, and we — our plans, our hopes, our aspirations and desires — fall short of complete fulfillment. Moses is not the one who brings us to the Promised Land, for he cannot enter himself.

No one can. That seems to be the message of the Torah, especially as it is experienced in the course of the yearly reading in the synagogue. Life is a long journey that ultimately is completed only in death. The goal of the journey, the final fulfillment of aspiration, is never achieved. Therefore, if satisfaction is to come in life, it must be in the course of life, in the choosing of life. There can be no other hope. In the traditional interpretation of the Torah, it is only in the connection to God achieved through the observance of the commandments and fulfillment of the covenant that we truly experience being alive. But, more than that, a reward for action or an ultimate accomplishment in life's work, cannot be expected.

This is a demanding spirituality. While there are moments of intimate contact with God that are described in the Torah, the hope for the layman, for the later reader of this text is limited, at best. "Choose life!" indeed, but is there no hope that in choosing life we will find some ease, some sense of accomplishment and rest? Although on some level it should be sufficient to strive to live out the call of God as presented in Torah, as difficult as that may be, the heart and soul yearn for more. Can we never go home? Shall we never arrive at "the rest and the inheritance that the Lord your God is giving you (Deut. 12:9)?" This question, this yearning, brings the reader with heart over and over again to the text, and finally reveals another answer: Yes.

This is *the Hebrew Book of the Dead*. Hidden in the biblical narrative, framed in the deep structure of the text, we find the lines of a different journey. At the same time that the Torah relates the travels of a man, his household, his descendants multiplied by ten thousand myriad, we also can read the story of the passage of the soul from its birth into this physical world of action through its death, shaking off the connection to the mundane to reconnect with the Eternal, prepared to return to the Land.

This teaching will differ significantly from the path of the Torah. There the national endeavor to keep the covenant supports and sustains the individual in his or her attempt to live through the commandments. This narrative will offer solace to the individual in the immediacy of each individual moment of each individual life. Life was met, even if death could not be defeated, in the act of fulfilling the covenant in the Torah. Life will be met and embraced, and death transcended, in *the Hebrew Book of the Dead*. The covenant that bound the People of Israel to its God in the Torah was formed at Sinai. In *the Hebrew Book of the Dead* the covenant that binds the soul in its body was cut in the flesh of Abraham and his descendants. The ideal of the Torah is to live to serve God through the commandments. The ideal in *the Hebrew Book of the Dead* is to serve God in joy; to live, so that one might come to love God.

These differences will be highlighted when we realize that *the Hebrew Book of the Dead* extends its view of the line of the narrative beyond the Five Books of Moses to include that of the Book of Joshua as well. The story does not end on the steppes of Moab, but in the entry into the

Land and the burial of the bones of Joseph in Shechem. In turn, this offers us a different understanding of the life and work of Moses. Where in the Torah he was the human, flesh-and-blood liberator of the Israelites, in *the Hebrew Book of the Dead* he is an angel, sent by God to liberate the soul from its earthly bondage. Moses' work is indeed complete when the journey through the wilderness is finished, since the renewed souls are ready to return from the World of Formation (Yetzirah) to the World of Making and Doing, the World of Action (Assiyah). Since he is an angel, and not of that latter world, Moses can take his leave of the People to remain in his proper domain. They will go forth to become flesh, to be circumcised into the covenant of life. He will stay behind, unbound by flesh, always present at the Sea of Ending to help lead the soul through the wilderness to again return to the World of Making at the River of Descent.

This is a completely different reading of Scripture. We have left the historical plane, the mundane world of land and inheritance, future and past, fear and fortune. We are now on the "spiritual" plane —at least in the sense of awareness of the breath as God's intimate presence, a presence bound also in the soul, which makes its way from one world to the next. The movement in the narrative is no longer geographical, it is spiritual. The movement of the soul is between spiritual realms, between the World of Formation (Yetzirah) and the World of Action (Assiyah).

The degree of intimacy with God, the level of awareness of God's infinite sustaining power, is greater in the former than the latter. The soul exists among, and is intimate with, angels in the World of Yetzirah. It then descends into the World of Assiyah, born into a body of flesh and blood and breath. The earlier awareness of a spiritual life, the consciousness of the soul of its divine quality is often obscured by the demands of human existence. Moments arise in which this can again be glimpsed, angels appear to remind us of our true nature, but we often miss them. The narrative of *the Hebrew Book of the Dead*, the passage of the soul from the World of Assiyah to the World of Yetzirah and back again, helps us to remember just those moments, reminds us to look for the angels. And, so, to deepen our awareness of God's presence in each moment of our lives, in every heartbeat and breath.

The soul descends into the world of doing, of physical actions and interactions, of hungers, passions and death. The locations on the ground are hints of the realms of experience of the soul. The descent of Joseph to Egypt is no longer the stuff of a novella, it is the movement of the soul deep into the physical world and its final rest in a coffin at death. The dramatic release of the enslaved Hebrews becomes the long-awaited release of the soul from the body to be raised up to the World of Formation, there to be renewed in the presence of angels. The long, conflict-filled and difficult passage through the wilderness is transformed into the complex process of the soul shaking off the vestiges of its physical attachments to learn again the immediate presence and power of God. The great celebration led by the priests at the crossing of the Jordan River and the covenant renewal at Gilgal describe the return of the soul to the World of Action, again to live out an embodied life, seeking to remember the presence of

God in each moment.

At the same time that the Torah relates the history of the People of Israel, it depicts the passage of every soul from the physical plane to the spiritual. Just as the text commands "Choose life!" and commands its readers to struggle, if only futilely, against death, it reassures them that death is not the end of experience. And, so, just as *the Hebrew Book of the Dead,* found under and around the text of the Torah, offers a story of the soul's renewal in the experience of God's immediate Presence, it offers hope to the readers of the Torah that God can be experienced even in the World of Doing.

What are the keys to the story told in this selection from *the Hebrew Book of the Dead?* One is the deep awareness of the unique nature of human creation. Bazak One, "Be Light," describing what was already ancient in its time, outlines the creation of the universe in ways that only today we realize are eerily close to modern scientific understandings. We now grasp that there is no real distinction between dust and stardust. On the quantum level, what we perceive to be the physical separation between palpable surfaces disappears. Nevertheless, we still marvel at our own beingness — ultimately our awareness of our existence, our consciousness. The Torah distinguishes human creation by attributing the divine image to the first beings. "Beloved are humans, in that they were created in the Divine Image. But, what great love was expressed, in that this knowledge was given to them (*Sayings of the Fathers, 3:14*)." But, deeper even than that is the presence of God's very breath in our nostrils. In Bazak Three, "A Living Soul," *the Hebrew Book of the Dead* focuses on what it was that brought the mud —dust and water — the human golem, into life. It is the presence of that breath that makes the body-and-soul of the human being "*Nefesh Chayyah*," a living being. Only because this spirit animates us, only because we have a divine soul, can we aspire to connect with the divine, to experience God's Presence.

We take for granted the dust and water that compose our physical beings. We trust our hearts to beat, our guts to digest and provide us with nourishment, our limbs to move at our will. We rarely wonder at the improbability that inanimate matter might actually transform other matter into energy, which in turn might make possible what we call life. We are but flesh and blood, dust and water, yet we are also *nefesh chayyah*, animate, conscious beings who carry God's presence in us in each and every breath. Each heartbeat sends out a new flood, recycling the primordial waters of Creation. Each breath returns to the body the spirit of God. In each moment, then, it should be possible to find God's Presence. Each moment can be another revelation. With each breath we can be created anew.

And so another key to understanding *the Hebrew Book of the Dead* is awareness of the moment. "Each moment, every second, we should take to heart that the Holy One, with great love and compassion, gives us renewed life, and each moment, every second, God creates us anew." We know this from the teaching in the midrash (*Gen. Rabbah 14:11*):

> Let every soul (*neshamah*) praise God (Psalms, 150:6)— with each and every breath (*neshimah*) praise God. Each moment, with

each exhalation, the soul seeks to leave the body. But the Holy One, with great mercy, protects us every second, and has compassion for us, and does not give leave to the soul to depart. Thus, we are created anew each moment, with every breath (Kedushat Levi, on Rosh HaShanah)."

This message is brought into sharp relief in Bazak Thirty-Nine of *the Hebrew Book of the Dead,*. "The Word." Here Senyak offers a vision of Deuteronomy 30:14 that is at once literal and transcendent. "For very near to you is the word, in your mouth and in your heart to do it (Deuteronomy, 30:14). " The experience of God's presence, the mercy and compassion of the Holy One, is possible every moment. The in-and-out of each breath, the pumping of the heart. Without much thought we take each breath. Without much attention we encounter and pass through each moment. Looking always ahead for the next thing to come, focused on whatever activity occupies our attention, the Presence of God slips by us unnoticed. We are left, often, with the sense that God is not present with us. Distracted as we are by our own endeavors and oblivious as we are to the immediate wonder of the intricate functioning of our bodies, we think that it must be difficult to find God. But, it is not hard. We need no one else, and we need not travel far or high to meet God in immediate experience. It is in our mouth — our breath — and in our hearts — the ongoing, untroubled, dependable beating — that we might meet God's presence.

A key to opening each moment, so that we can meet

the present in its immediacy, is to learn to pay attention. Each breath and each moment passes so quickly. We must withdraw for a moment, ever so slightly, from the hurly-burly of our daily affairs, from the distractions of the moment, to find a place of solitude and quiet. This is the setting for Bazak Forty, "Choose Life," where Moses, hidden in the cleft of the rock, experiences the rushing flow of God's Presence. His experience affirms the impossibility of holding on to the passage of time. We cannot see God's face, but we can experience God's Presence in the moment, see, as it were, God's back. This, too, was Elijah's experience in the cave in the wilderness. He, too, needed solitude to clarify his mind, to focus his attention, to allow him to realize how close indeed is that "still, small voice" beating in his chest, in each and every moment.

This retreat, this quest for a solitude that would allow us to sense God's Presence might lead us all out into the wilderness. We might all become hermits. But the earth was made for us to inhabit, for it is in the world, in the very substance and workings of Creation that we find God: "I am the Lord, and there is none else." And yet the world is so attractive, it demands so much of our attention, that we are often distracted from the ongoing wonder of the moment-by-moment renewal of all existence, and we find it difficult to sense God's Presence in the midst of it all.

And, so, we are left, seemingly, with only two options: willful abandonment of God or absolute self-annihilating devotion. In Bazak Thirty, "The Slave," the *Hebrew Book of the Dead* turns to the body of law known as the Covenant Code, the Scripture that follows the Ten Commandments. The first of the rules in this code has to do with the laws of the Hebrew slave. Such indentured servants must be liberated after six years. Circumstances may demand that one relinquish freedom, but the true and full service of the Holy One demands our free devotion and full attention. There are those slaves who may choose to remain slaves. Choose not to be free. What could be so attractive, so insistent, that it would seduce one away from freedom, from the full possibility of serving the God who brought us out of the land of Egypt, the house of bondage? "I love my master and my wife and children" (Exodus 21:5). Social interaction, the most elemental of human experiences; connection to spouse, to offspring, to neighbor tie us securely to the matters of this world. A door was opened for him to go, to find a moment of silence, of freedom from outside distraction, and he refused to go to meet God.

That is the way for most of us. Doors are opened before us — "it is in your mouth and your heart to do it" — and we refuse to pass through. We allow distraction and attachment to close us off from the immediate experience of God's Presence. We often choose this over the constant struggle to disengage, to remember that above and below the clamoring of family, work, and community, that within each moment accompanied by the love and care of family, is the passing moment. It would be possible to grasp that moment, even when we love our master, our wife, and our children, but it is difficult. Most of us fall into habit, close off our ears, and lose touch with the breath in our nostrils and the pounding in our chests. And then we call out, "Why, O Lord, do You stand so far

179

away? "(Psalms 10:1)

The other extreme in this polarity is to give oneself over to God fully, with abandon, without care or concern for anything of this physical world. It is to seek to come as close to God as possible, to enter fully into God's realm. This level of devotion is not easily attained, nor sustained. It is so fully focused on the presence of God, so totally aware that "there is none else," that nothing truly exists but God, that it completely effaces physical reality. The bright light of God's being nullifies all else.

This light is represented in the fire that descends to consume the offerings of Aaron and his sons at the dedication of the Tabernacle and their installation as priests. That same fire burns in all of us. It is the oxidizing process that ultimately wears us out, that devours our bodies and removes us from the world. We embrace that subtle flame, blindly, selfishly, for it warms our bodies and provides energy to do our work. We ignore the fact that it is burning us up in the process.

In Bazak Thirty-three, "Strange Fire," *the Hebrew Book of the Dead* draws near the ultimate instance of *devekuth*, single-minded devotion, found in the Bible. Nadav and Avihu, Aaron's older sons, realized that the flame that burned inside them was the flame that burned on the altar. They understood that any distinction they might make between these fires would only separate them from the source of the flame, from the presence of God. So, they filled their firepans, offered incense, expressed their burning inner desire to come close to God, to rise up into God's embracing being and become one with God. And, they succeeded.

And fire came forth from the Lord and con-

sumed them; thus they died at the instance of
the Lord. Then Moses said to Aaron, "This is
what the Lord meant when He said:
'Through those near to Me I show Myself
holy, and gain glory before all the people.'"
(Leviticus, 10:2-3).

Their devotion was all consuming. They forsook all,
even their physical lives, to approach God, to draw near,
and to glorify the Holy One.

Such devotion is beyond most of us in this world, at
least until the last moment. "Rabbi Eliezer taught: repent,
turn back to God, one day before your death Avot 2:
10)." Even if we were to live our lives completely
thoughtless of God and oblivious to God's presence, we
might yet open ourselves to that experience, even at the
last moment. It is not merely repentance for sins that
Rabbi Eliezer urges upon us. It is a return to our quest to
know God, to experience that presence in our mouths
and hearts. It is to open our hearts to such passion, such
devotion to God, that we, like Nadav and Avihu, relinquish our bodies to meet God fully in the moment.

We can realize the approach of death, and rather than
resist, rather than hold onto our master, our wife, our
children, we can let go. "There is none else" — the curtain that we draw between us and God that allows us to
take a wife and job, to nail our ears to the doorpost, can
be withdrawn. We can step back and acknowledge that all
that we have done, all that we have accomplished is nothing more than one small contribution to the infinite ways
in which the Holy One is manifested in the world of doing. We did not do anything. Our accomplishments were

not for us. They were for God's glory, for they were God's glory. What do we wish to hold on to that we can truly claim belongs to us? Nothing, not even that with which we are most intimate, our bodies. In that last day, in the last moment, we can give over and let go, and release ourselves wholeheartedly into the streaming moment of God's presence. In that moment we gain eternity, the fact of our approaching death is diminished in importance and our despair at death vanishes like smoke.

The capacity to let go of the body and embrace fully the Presence of God, without any intervening curtains or distracting attachments, is the ultimate expression of freedom. It is release from bondage to the physical as well as the emotional. It is worthy of our attention in this life, but it is the essential element of the journey of the soul from this world to the next. We learn the former from the latter when we read *the Hebrew Book of the Dead*, just as we learn all of the other elements of our spiritual quest. The importance of this reading of the Torah is that it brings to the fore that which had been hidden. It allows us to remember that the Torah is not only a history or law-code, nor only a tribal epic or constitution. We are reminded that it is not only a resource for examining the psychological dynamics of families and tribes, or gaining insight into our own relationships with family, friends, and community. Reading *the Hebrew Book of the Dead* is to recall that among all of the other possibilities the Torah is a spiritual guide for the soul.

As we learn about the renewal of the soul in its journey through the wilderness finally to be reborn, through the River of Descent, to Gilgal and finally in a body at Shechem, we learn also of its journey in the World of Action.

182

The same servitude and blindness that prevent the soul from being shriven of its earthly attachments in the World to Come are those that interfere with our experiencing God in the course of our lives in this World. In a sense, the life of the World of Action is a mirror image of the life of the soul in its passage from one life to the next. And, as with all images, we prefer the item to its reflection. However full the spiritual quest may be in this realm, it is still far short of the experience of the soul in its next stage, following our death. Nevertheless, it is in this life that we read both the Torah and *the Hebrew Book of the Dead*, and so it is in this life that we struggle to learn the lessons of both, and seek to see God's face, to feel God's presence.

My interest in *the Hebrew Book of the Dead* was first sparked by the challenge of re-reading a familiar text in a new light. As a modern Conservative rabbi, my eyes were trained to interpret in particular ways, my heart was inclined to understand the text in certain ways, and my ears heard the text in familiar ways. Although midrash as a form of text interpretation was a known and beloved companion, this reading of Torah seemed different, more challenging, less susceptible to historical, political, or communal contextualization. Like looking at an optical trick, where the hidden image moves in and out of perception, at times what Zhenya Senyak put before me stood out clearly, and at others it was obscure. At times I thought I was being invited to participate in a personal mental game – can you see this message behind these words? can I translate this word in this manner and still remain true to the text? Over time I came to recognize the

183

overarching coherence of the interpretation, I began to hear the deep personal struggle being worked out in the book, and I felt the spiritual power that this telling had to offer.

Serving a congregation in a large community with a small Jewish population, I was leery of the argument regarding reclaiming the use of the Divine Name YHVH. Too many of my Christian colleagues used it too familiarly, too colloquially. I felt both that they were taking my God too lightly, and that in their familiarity they were taking my God. Among Jews, to preserve its power and to maintain its mystery, the Name has been held with such distant regard. To employ it as a way of talking about "Israel's God" diminished it, denied my sense of that God's very presence on every page of Torah, in my daily prayers, in my life. I would not jump easily at the call to reclaim its use.

And, while I still would not advocate its casual use or cease to use the various circumlocutions that have evolved over the years (they are so dear, so intimate), I have been moved by the argument in Bazak Twenty-one of *the Hebrew Book of the Dead,* "The Name," that not only have we substituted one word in place of another, we have actually stopped seeing the original. The loss of intimacy with the YHVH name, with its connection to the Name Eheyeh-asher-eheyeh of the burning bush, has come at a spiritual cost. We are less in touch with, less in the presence of the Eternal One, the One of Being-and-Becoming, the Eternal Present. YHVH is much less a name than onomatopoeia — an attempt to speak the very nature of being, to breathe into word the essence of existence. But, over time, it has indeed become a stable, fixed placeholder for all of the other locutions by which we seek to speak of God. It is no longer dynamic, and so it can no longer move those who would dance with it, engage with the God who is embodied in it.

That argument of *the Hebrew Book of the Dead* caught my ear. It called me to look again at the whole of the book, and to consider what it had to offer to me, to my congregants, to other spiritual seekers. I read it again and found myself quaking in the cleft in the rock. I found myself with my ear pressed hard against the doorpost. I went up with Joseph's bones and descended again, riding the wheel of Gilgal. I found myself newly minted, circumcised again to enter into the life of this world, only to descend into the pit once more. And, I found that, rather than a sentence of death, being a *nefesh chayyah,* a living being, was an invitation to full appreciation of God's Presence in me, in every moment.

This is a powerful message. It is different from the message of awareness of God's presence, or attainment to holiness through the recitation of blessings or the performance of commandments. It is different from the message of classical reward and punishment, or the contemporary sense of the act is its own reward. Freed from the fears of the accidents of this life, freed also from the limitations of human existence and finitude, I could reclaim a connection to the Eternal. Even if only for a moment, for one breath at a time, I could enter into the flow of the Eternal One, remember that "it is in your mouth and your heart to do it."

This is no escape from the truth of human existence. "This is the teaching of man: he will die" still applies. I will still love, and so give myself over to being enslaved. I will lust after cucumbers and leeks, remembering how good the pleasures of the flesh are. I will fear that silence means absence, and so I will create my own golden calf to protect me from my own weakness and failures. I will resist that which is difficult, choosing instead to blame others, looking like grasshoppers in my own eyes, and therefore I must look so to others. And, I will suffer, for all of this will lead to loss. I will lose sight of God. I will sense that I am at the farthest ends of the world and that God is as distant from me as sunrise is from sunset.

But, the key to release is close, as close as my breath, as intimate as my heartbeat. In just a moment of silence, of stepping out of the rush of life, I can reclaim a sense of God's presence. This will not end the suffering, but it will limit its power over me. If I can climb out of the pit, if I can recognize angels accompanying me, if I can come up for air, I can break the hold of despair and reclaim God's Presence and love. In addition, this perspective offers additional resources to work to end the suffering of all. That "you were a slave in the land of Egypt" is not only a justification for an action, nor mere motivational speech. It is experience. I am liberated with each breath. I am freed in each moment I give myself over to God, and shake off the hold of servitude. I can know directly God's saving power in each moment, since I am created anew, and so I am not bound by my past, I can change. That is liberation. And I will want to share that with everyone. I will not rest seeing others suffer. My liberation will empower me, it will challenge me, it will call me to work for the liberation of all others.

My path is not that of Nadav and Avihu. "I will not

die, but live, that I might tell of the mighty works of God" (Psalms, 118:17). Self-sacrifice may be a way of liberation, but I cannot choose it. It is not my way, and I do not think that it will appeal to most others. But, that is what we need today — a message that will inspire, that will help all seekers to find their way to God. It is the possibility that *the Hebrew Book of the Dead* and what it brings alive in the Torah might inspire my congregants and make them seekers that moved me to join Zhenya Senyak in bringing this book to the larger community.

May we all merit a moment in which we experience in all its goodness the presence of God pass us by as we find our own cleft in the rock, there to find liberation, and peace.

— *Rabbi Jonathan P. Slater*
Hastings-on-Hudson, New York

Appendix A
The Song of Ascents
Psalms of Transformation

A young rabbi in Berkeley, California wrote me of his readings in *Tehillim*, the biblical Book of Psalms. As a chaplain, he wrote, he often sat at the bedside of the gravely ill and found himself comforting survivors.

He found himself drawn to one section, the Song of Ascents. In these psalms he found an echo of the journey told in *the Hebrew Book of the Dead,* the rising of the soul from the pit to cross the wilderness into the Promised Land.

In the course of time we lost touch, and now I cannot recall his name. Perhaps, in the sense that we are all angels to one another, he is simply an angel who arose to deliver this message.

During this period, accompanying a dying loved person, I remembered the Song of Ascents and started working with it with my rebbe, HaRanit. Since then I have shared it with a few people, finding it a powerful tool of transformation, capable of guiding and comforting a troubled soul through difficult times. In crossing critical passages in a life, illness, and death or simply profound changes brought by age and circumstance, the Song of Ascents is an unfailing companion.

The Song of Ascents is a small book within the Book of Psalms. It is made up of fifteen brief psalms, each of which starts *shir ha'ma'alote.* The psalms — numbers 120-134 — taken together and in sequence may be read as songs ascending, with the human Soul, from her time of disincarnation through to unification in God. They may also be read as stations in a journey from despair to joy.

Ha'-ma'aloth is from the Hebrew, *aliyah,* meaning to ascend, to go up. The burnt offering at the Temple was called the *olah* because it went up to God. The Israelites going to Jerusalem, the exiles returning to Israel from Babylon, go up to the land, make *aliyah.* And when the body dies, the soul is lifted up, returned in a series of risings up to its origins in the great *aliyah* of ending its journey incarnate on Earth.

Just as there are fifteen *aliyoth* or Songs of Ascent in the Book of Psalms, the rabbis note there were fifteen steps in the Temple leading to the Court of the Israelites. It is written that on Succoth, at the place of the Water Drawing during the Ceremony of Rejoicing, the Levites stood on those fifteen steps and sang the Song of Ascents.

The music of these sweet songs is a powerful companion to the soul in times of trial. From the opening cry of pain to the concluding song in the cycle, "Behold, the Lord," step by step, the Song of Ascents traces the path of the soul's redemption.

In this setting, each song of the ascents, as revealed in the teachings of HaRanit, is framed by a brief title and a single line from the psalm. Reading the full text of the complete cycle, aloud and with deep *kavanah,* carries the spirit up, step by step, to joyous reunion.

The Song of Ascents
שיר המעלות
Shir ha'ma'aloth

First Aliyah - Distress - Psalm 120
In my distress I called upon the Lord and He answered me.

אל־יי" בצרתה לי קראתי ויענני
El-YHVH batzaratah li karati vaya'anayyni

Second Aliyah- Hope- Psalm 121
I will lift up my eyes to the mountains from where my help comes.

אשא עיני אל־ההרים מאין יבא עזרים
Esa einai el heharim meiayin yavo ezri

Third Aliyah - Rising Up - Psalm 122
Let us go up to the house of the Lord

בית י" נלך
Bayt YHVH naylech

Fourth Aliyah - Supplication -Psalm 123
Be gracious unto us Lord, be gracious unto us.

חננו יהוה חננו
Chanaynu YHVH, chanaynu

Fifth Aliyah - Deliverance -Psalm 124

If the Lord were not with us…the raging waters would have gone over our soul.

לולי י" שהיה לנו אזי עבר על־נפשנו המים
הזידונים

*Lulai YHVH shehiyah lahnu…ahzi ahvar al-nafshaynu
ha'mayim ha'zaydonim*

Sixth Aliyah - Attachment -Psalm 125

They that join themselves to the Lord..abide forever

הבטחים בי" לעולם ישב

Ha'botechim b'YHVH l'olam yeshev

Seventh Aliyah - Jubilation - Psalm 126

We were as dreamers

היינו כחלמים

Hayinu c'cholmeem

Eighth Aliyah - Submission - Psalm 127

If the Lord does not build the house…

אם־י" לא־יבנה בית

Im-YHVH lo-yivneh bahyit

Ninth Aliyah- Joy in Submission - Psalm 128

Happy are all who fear the Lord, the walker on His path.

אשרי כל־ירא י" החלך בדרכיו

Ashrei kol-yirah YHVH, hacholech be'ad'rachaf

Tenth Aliyah - Contemplation - Psalm 129
The plowers plowed upon my back
על־גבי חרשו חרשים
Al-gabi charshu chorshim

Eleventh Aliyah- Forgiveness - Psalm 130
For with You is forgiveness
כי־עמך הסליחה
Ki imcha ha'slichah

Twelfth Aliyah- Comfort - Psalm 131
My soul is with me like a weaned child.
כגמל עלי נפשי
K'gamul ahlie nafshi

Thirteenth Aliyah - Homecoming - Psalm 132
Here is my restingplace forever; Here will I dwell
זות־מנוחתי עדי־עד פו אשב
Zote menuchati adei-ad po eishev

Fourteenth Aliyah - Unification -Psalm 133
Behold how good and pleasant it is
הנה מה־תוב ומה־נעים
Hinei mah tov umah-naaim

Fifteenth Aliyah - Rapture - Psalm 134
Behold, Bless the Lord all Servants of God.
הנה ברכו את־י" כל־עבדי י"
Hinei barchu et-YHVH kol-avdi YHVH

The Fifteen Stages of Ascent

The Songs of Aliyah

1. Distress   Psalm 120
The end time of the body. Confusion and pain.
2. Hope   Psalm 121
Glimpses of the light.
3. Rising up   Psalm 122
On the final breath, the *ruach* slips back into the ocean of
Spirit, starting the soul's disincarnation. *Aliyah.*

The Songs of Crossing the Sea

4. Supplication   Psalm 123
A cry for support in the uprising of the spirit.
5. Deliverance   Psalm 124
Understanding that the waters shall be held surely apart
and the soul is delivered from chaos and darkness.
6. Attachment   Psalm 125
Deep attachment to the source of life that draws the soul
on.

7. Jubilation   Psalm 126
Great joy at surviving the passage between the waters into
the World of Yetzirah, the unfolding desert wilderness.

The Songs of Redemption

8. Submission   Psalm 127
Release of personality.
9. Joy in Submission   Psalm 128
Joyful acceptance of the soul's path.
10. Contemplation   Psalm 129
The final look back, review of life incarnate.
11. Forgiveness   Psalm 130
Cleansing of sin, acceptance into the path of the Lord.

The Songs of Rapture

12. Comfort   Psalm 131
Sense of well-being, ease.
13. Homecoming   Psalm 132
Sense of timelessness, rest.
14. Unification   Psalm 133
Companionship of kindred spirits.
15. Rapture   Psalm 134
Thinning of the veils, opening to
the light.

Appendix B

A Hidden Book of the Dead in the Hebrew Bible.

The Ancient Hebrews, the Hebrew nomadic tribes-people who lived the biblical stories — and the settled Hebrew dwellers in Canaan who wrote those stories —are both core to Western Civilization and deeply hidden from us by time and myth.

Like all ancient civilizations, their closest beliefs are shrouded in a soft darkness that no archeological dig can unearth: conversations around desert campfires, up-welling of terror and ecstasy in the hearts of men, women, and children in their houses, on their pilgrimages, in time of war and time of peace. Their central beliefs are revealed in the Torah, their most ancient writings.

From these scrolls, and other physical evidence, we know something of them: The Ancient Hebrews were sharp, pragmatic survivors, frequently banded together against common enemies but equally ready to fight one another over land and rights. They lived in one of the world's toughest neighborhoods, a hot, arid, and contentious place, flattened by the Sun. It was a place where powerful enemy kings took slaves and put out the eyes of enemies, salted the conquered earth, and exacted heavy tribute from common people and princes, alike.

For a brief period they carved out a Kingdom between the Sea and the River. By the time they built a Temple to YHVH in Jerusalem, the Hebrews were ancient no longer, but firmly anchored in history.

We do them a disservice in perpetuating myths of their credulity. Hard-boiled and tenacious, they were sharp immigrants clawing their way into the Promised Land.

The Ancient Hebrews were a most unlikely horde to be the bearers of ecstatic news, seers and poets, and yet they were. In this harsh land, these people knew angels intimately and came into the Courts of the King to learn compassion and justice, to cherish community and freedom. Out of the marauding wanderings of the Ancient Hebrews came a direct, mystical view of reality and a stubborn, incandescent love of YHVH.

Simply, somewhere along the way, something happened. Something happened in the formative years before the Israelite conquest of Canaan that set these people afire. They marched with legions of Angels.

The most comprehensive record of the Ancient Hebrews is the Bible. By reading the Bible closely, in Hebrew — and relating that reading to surrounding historical events — it becomes possible to illuminate some of the darkness surrounding the ideas and beliefs of these people. What emerges in the heart of the Torah, is *the Hebrew Book of the Dead.*

The *Hebrew Book of the Dead* is a reading of Hebrew Scripture that tells, in literal translation, the story of the passage of a single soul between lives. All the Hebrew sourcetext comes directly from the Torah and the Book of Joshua. The central idea: Within Scripture there is a clearly defined book of the dead hidden by translation and tradition.

There is ample linguistic, historic, and metalinguistic evidence to help unearth this Book of the Dead from the most ancient Hebrew writings.

Linguistic Evidence

Three main linguistic elements helped uncover this book. The first concerns the entrance of the Hebrew tribes into the Desert Wilderness, the second, their exit forty years later, and the third element illuminates their first destination in the Promised Land.

Entrance: The Yam Sof

To enter the Desert Wilderness, the Hebrews cross the *YAM SOF,* the Sea of "*SOF.*" Although traditionally mis-translated as The Red Sea, the *YAM SOF* could be (1) the Sea of Reeds but is more likely (2) the Sea of Ending (or the Extremity of the Earth, as used in Daniel 4:8) or (3) the Sea of Perishing (Psalms 73:19, Esther 9:28).

Despite their semantic differences, all these words are phonetically and morphemically identical: *SOF* = Samekh Vav Pey, **סוף.** And, by far, in Hebrew Scripture, the more common meaning of the form *SOF* has to do with "Ending," rather than "Reeds."

First linguistic point: The fleeing Hebrews, with Moses and the bones of Joseph, arrive at the Sea of Ending. What has ended? Joseph's life — and long period of waiting for his bones to be carried up across the desert — and their own slavery has ended. What is beginning? The journey across the wilderness to revelation, purification, freedom and a new life in the Promised Land is beginning.

Exit: The Jordan River

Across the Desert Wilderness, forty years later, awaits the Jordan ירדן River, and about the meaning of this word there is no argument. The root means "Descend," or "go down." ירד, Yod Reysh Dalet, is always used in this precise sense.

Second linguistic point: To leave the Desert Wilderness, the bones of Joseph must descend to a Lower World, must be carried across The Waters of Descent to re-enter the flesh.

Destination - Gilgal

The first destination in the Promised Land is *Gilgal,* the Wheel, the Hebrew word for reincarnation.

And the people came up out of Jordan on the tenth day of the first month, and encamped in Gilgal, in the east border of Jericho (Joshua, 4:19).

The issue of reincarnation is central to *the Hebrew Book of the Dead* and is, in fact, the point of the journey across the desert wilderness: to become free in order to descend into the flesh in the World of Assiyah to do the work of YHVH. There are allusions to reincarnation in the Torah, throughout the Hebrew Bible, and in the Talmud. Josephus, in *Antiquities* 18:1 and in *Jewish Wars* 2:8, refers to reincarnation.

In any case, it is certain that by the post-talmudic period the doctrine of Gilgal, or transmigration of souls, was accepted by the Karaites. By the time the *Bahir* was published in the Twelfth Century, it was taken for granted, and the concept has been central to all forms of the Kabbalah.

Third linguistic point: The first stop for the purified *Nefesh* after crossing the River of Descent is Gilgal, reincarnation.

About the destination of the Hebrews crossing the Wilderness, there is another, significant linguistic point appearing in Bazak Seventeen, "A Tree of Death." Joseph's bones, carried up from his grave and taken across the desert wilderness, are called עצמות *aytzmot*, or skeleton. *Aytz Mot* is literally Tree of Death and, in light of the opening of Genesis, where the Tree of Life is planted in the center of the Garden of Eden, and the end of Joshua, where Joseph's Tree of Death is placed in the ground in the Promised Land, this framing device seems more than coincidental.

The Historic Context

Beyond semantic and morphological data, there are historical reasons to believe a central portion of the Hebrew Torah contains a Book of the Dead. The Hebrews arose in a part of the world where the dead were worshiped, where other cultures had produced earlier books of the dead, most notably *The Egyptian Book of the Dead*. The many correspondences between the Ugaritic texts, the wars of Baal and Mot in the Underworld, and the Hebrew Bible have been long known. Within Ugarit, a very ancient northern Canaanite city located in today's Syria, there was a cult of the dead. (This is not surprising since the city was under Egyptian hegemony from at least 1800 to 1400 B.C.E.) Two stela found in Ugarit refer to the dead as *rephaim*, the same term used by Isaiah (14:9).

Nor were Hebrews themselves immune to these practices, as witnessed by I Samuel: 28, "And Saul said, 'Bring me up Samuel.'"

The historical evidence for Hebrew assimilation of some practices of their host cultures supports the idea that the early Hebrews did indeed incorporate material from dominant Middle Eastern cultures into their own stories and writings. Belief in life after death in some Sheol or Hades, and reincarnation, as well as books of the dead were commonplace in the ancient Near and Middle East.

Some Metalinguistic Evidence

Finally, there are seven compelling metalinguistic reasons to believe *the Hebrew Book of the Dead* is the central story of the Torah. These all focus on the Desert Wilderness:

1. The bones of Joseph (*Asaph=* Carried Off, *Gen. 30:23*) are carried up by Moses and brought through the Sea of Ending, across the *midbar*, through the Waters of De-

scent to Reincarnation in the Promised Land. This is simply literal translation of the Hebrew text.

2. Characteristics of life in the Desert Wilderness, the *midbar*, have an ethereal quality, strongly suggestive of a World of the Spirit separated from the Body:

There is no struggle to obtain food, for manna is available on the ground, food dropping from Heaven not growing from the earth

There is no struggle to find shelter from the sun or cold.

No one is conceived and born in the midbar in all the forty years of wandering. (There are sixty-seven "begats" in Genesis, none in Exodus.)

3. The waters split on both sides of the *midbar* to permit passage of the Hebrews. The interpretation that these are birth waters opening to reveal the *yavashar* —the virgin earth upon which no foot has trod before — gains power from other instances of the waters opening. The separation of the waters occurs in the opening of Genesis (1:9) as an act of Creation. The waters separate at the Sea of Ending as the fleeing Hebrews, carrying the bones of Asaph, spill into the desert wilderness. And, in Joshua, the Levites carry the Ark of the Word through the parted Jordan River, the Waters of Descent, so the children of Israel may start their new life in the Promised Land.

4. The *Nefesh* is born into the flesh. This act is acknowledged by the circumcision at Gilgal and the end of the period of manna, once the new-born living being eats the food of the Promised Land (Joshua 5:2, 5:12).

5 From the time the bones of Asaph are carried into the Wilderness, the Hebrews face trial after trial in which love for God is pitted against material desires, longing for familiar foods, for life in the flesh, for meat, cucumbers and relish. It is a longing that pits the spirit against the flesh, the Mud Man against the *ruach,* and leads directly to the worship of the golden calf at the foot of the mountain.

6. Only after the epiphany of Strange Fire (Bazak Thirty-three, Lev.10) does the wandering Soul become purified and set out, again, across the *midbar* to the Promised Land. In Leviticus the sons of the High Priest sacrifice themselves to atone for the sin of the golden calf. It is here that the metalinguistic meets the purely linguistic, for the sons who are willing sacrifices for the sins of their father and the community are called Nadav (Willing) and Avihu (He-is-my-father).

7. Although portions of *the Hebrew Book of the Dead* extend through the whole Torah and the Book of Joshua, the very great bulk of the book is taken from שמות *Shemot*, the Book of Names, Exodus. And here it should be noted the word *Shemot* itself may be yet another pointer to this hidden book. For while שמות Shem-ot unquestionably means "Names," the identical form שמות sh-Mot is translated "of death."

Appendix C

On Worlds & Sephirot

The Hebrew Book of the Dead commentary contains many allusions to the Worlds and to Sephirot. These kabbalist concepts, articulated between the time of the Hebrew Scriptures and our own Post-Modern era, are useful to visualize dynamic states of Divine emanation.. This appendix was requested by early readers who believed a brief introduction to the major elements of this world view would useful to readers of the Commentary in this book. For those who want a more detailed, comprehensive look at the Sephirot and Worlds, many excellent sources exist. First among these would be Gershom G. Scholem's landmark study, Major Trends in Jewish Mysticism (Schocken) *and Adin Steinsalz' Thirteen Petalled Rose* (BasicBooks). *Personal favorites include the highly illustrated Charles Poncé's* Kabbalah (*Straight Arrow), Henri Sérouya's* La Kabbale *(Grasset) and Daniel Matt's* The Essential Kabbalah (*Castle Books). - ZS*

There is a place that does not exist, whose coordinates cannot be plotted, whose description is utterly artificial, and yet our journey toward it brings us to the Court of the King.

When we arrive at the foot of the Throne, however, we have achieved nothing and reached no place, for all things change continually. In a moment we are infinitely far from the Source of Being, plunged into darkness. Turn around and we are home, briefly. On this journey, the most pious and exalted among us stand most in danger of darkest exile and the most degraded and humiliated stand closest to the Throne.

This dance of life and death is in our breath, *karov me'od.* Very near.

We breathe in our life and breathe out our death. We suck in the *ruach* of the universe and release the products of our own combustion back into the cosmos, in and out all our days, never reaching a place where we no longer need to breathe at all.

Our expiration is always accompanied by the release of a final breath, and on that breath we travel. We can no longer return to that garment of our soul that remains, inert, behind us. On this new journey, again we will be formed and destroyed, for the implacable path of Creation leaves destruction in its wake. And builds life from destruction. Even in the dark bowels of destruction, in the dense black holes in the Universe, life springs forth under the spell of Creation.

At all times, we have the power to feel this flow. We can stop and be quiet. We breathe. We feel the breath entering the body, filling the lungs, building excitement and tension. And then we feel the breath leaving, the relaxation and quiet. Life and death in the body of a human being.

We are glorious, gluttonous human beings traveling up and down the days of life, breathing in and out, from youth to decrepitude, breathing. In and out, up and down.

There is a kabbalistic structure that puts all this together in an elegant geometry that is endless in its beauty and complexity. It is the Tree of Life that extends through all the Worlds. It is a Tree made up of ten Sephirot and it does not exist beyond the human mind.

Sephirot, from the Hebrew "number," represent spheres of God's unfolding Presence, the unfolding potencies of the *Ayn Sof,* the Eternal. The ten Sephirot are Keter (Crown), Chochmah (Wisdom), Binah (Understanding), Chesed (Lovingkindness), Din (Judgment, Power), Tiferet (Beauty), Netzah (Victory, Endurance), Hod (Majesty), Yesod (Foundation), and Malchut (Kingdom, the Shekkinah).

At the head of the Tree is the Sephirah Keter, the Crown, the brilliant diadem that sits on the head of the created world. It is all things glorious and unattainable. The Creator, passing by in the night, strolling in the Garden, sways the branches of the Tree of Life in the golden evening breezes, leaving a flake of Glory on its crowning leaves. Keter is the first Sephirah.

At the Tree's base is the tenth Sephirah, Malchut, the Kingdom. This Sephirah rules the World of Assiyah, the material World of Action, of making and doing. Commonly, Sephirah Malchut is known as the home of the Shekkinah, the Feminine side of Be-ing. For many, Malchut is the Goddess, the nurturing body from which all things come.

Crown and Kingdom, they cannot exist without each other. The polarity of this Tree, the positive/negative charge, is top and bottom, King and Queen, male and female, the in and out twirling of exploding, swirling universes.

In our passage through the Worlds, we find ourselves in all parts of the Tree, but, at various times, we come under the influence of one or more Sephirot. It is a way to look at our condition, a way to explore the influences at work in our lives.

The Tree of Life is meant to be a map of God's emanation from Creation to our created life in the World of Making, in Assiyah. The basic structure of the Tree has three columns, one central and one on either side, right and left, male and female, expansion and contraction. The first three Sephirot, one Sephirah from each column, together express the highest World, the World of Atzilut. From these three upper Sephirot are generated the lower seven Sephirot, two groups of three Sephirot plus Malchut.

The first two lower Sephirot are Chesed and Din. (Traditionally, they are the result of the union of Chochmah and Binah.) The union of Chesed and Din produces Tifereth, the Sephirah that rules the heart of the Tree. Taken together, these three Sephirot express the emanation of the World of Beriah, the World of Creation.

Thus, through action, reaction and synthesis do the Sephirot unroll dialectically through the Tree of Life, from the Crown to Kingdom, from God to the Shekkinah. And as powers emanate down the through the Tree, so too do actions generate influences that move up the Tree.

In practical terms, The Tree is a path, a chart of our days that can be used to consider global spiritual positioning as well as our own personal place in events   For example, to achieve balance between compassion and discipline, between Chesed and Din, is to produce a life of Tifereth. This is one ideal emerging from this image. But in these days we live near the surface of Din, and our times are harsh in judgment, closed-minded and filled with rigor. The world's hard-won scientific achievements and our barbaric genocides alike come from Din.

Crossing from the Kingdom to the Crown, or moving in the opposite direction, there is a time in our journey that we cross the valley between *Din* and *Chesed*. Sometimes, when we are sitting quietly feeling the sweet ruach feeding our Soul, we can let our minds travel through the Sephirot and discover the place prepared for us for this time. All the Sephirot are material for meditation and transformation, rich in imagery, complex, spiritual passageways along the way. These are representations of Emanations and Realms of God, but they are only the work of human hands for all that. Like art, in any form, they can serve to open the human heart. The great danger is they may also be set up as a golden calf.

Frequently, kabbalists map the Sephirot to the Four Worlds. The World of Emanation, Atziluth, is the locus of Keter, Chochmah and Binah; the World of Creation, Beriah, is the divine manifestation of Chesed, Gevurah, and Tifereth. The World of Formation, Yetzirah, the setting of *the Hebrew Book of the Dead* and the domain of Angels, is characterized by the next trine of Sephirot: Netzah, Hod, and Yesod. In our World of Action, the World of Assiyah, God's immanence is expressed through the Sephirah of Malchut, the Kingdom, to which all emanations flow.

In a popular kabbalist variation, the Tree is repeated in each World. That is, all ten Sephirot exist in each World with the Malchut of the higher World becoming the Keter of the lower.

The danger in learning even this nomenclature is to think we know anything at all. While the power of this image of the Tree of Life derives from deep mystical truth, Tiferet is not a place or a thing. There is no Crown of gold, no Kingdom. In a world where God may not be pictured, the kabbalistic construction of four Worlds and ten Sephirot is a rich system of imagery. Although Tiferet may not in fact exist, any more than those whirling electron rings around the nucleus of an atom, or the number two, it reflects a profound and useful reality to seekers on the path.

To start the journey to God having faith only in the journey itself, only in God, means to live right here in the Present streaming moment. And in that process, names and Trees alike fall away before the Light.

We know nothing at all. And in that is all our freedom. We need only listen to our breaths, hear our heart's beat — pumping the red *ruach* through our blue starved blood — to come back to God. *Devka-bo*. Cling to Him, said the Angel Mosheh. We will not always succeed for we are all Mud Beings, spirits in bodies of leek-loving flesh, but reunited in YHVH is our true life. We can try continually to practice *devekuth*, or we can argue our theories of crowns and kings and sephirotic systems and lose our soul in our introspections.

The greater awakening is in this realization: All

that matters is where we are right now, at this instant, in our relationship to God. Is the Lord of Be-ing blazing before our eyes, burning in our hearts, or are we to talk about God as if YHVH were some kind of parlor trick, able to be summoned and displayed to the astonishment of our friends?

Are we on our way up the mountain to that craggy split where, perched and trembling, we will await the Lord, or are we permanently settled in our base camp, checking our equipment, studying maps and talking about climbs we made in the past?

We cannot open our hearts and close our minds at the same time. That is the Way of the Fanatic, the Way of Delusion. To know God, we must open all our being to the flow of infinite light filtering through all the Worlds. It is here the Tree of Life, by providing a ladder of transformation, transcends its fictional state. Though the work of our hands, the Sephirot and all the Worlds reflect the awe and glory of Creation.

Devka-Bo. Cling to Him. That is all the objective of our lives in this World.

For some, the Sephirot are one means to arrive at *devekuth.* There are times we all simply forget to follow our breath and are too jangled to meditate. If we can be still, and remember to breathe, our intricate journeys through the Sephirot can take us, again, to the foot of the Throne where we may sense the glinting gold of the Crown, infinitely far away yet, once again, *karov me'od,* very near.

Kabbalist Notebook
How to Find God

The *Hebrew Book of the Dead* is an ancient Hebrew vision of God and the human journey across Worlds after death.

This same vision extends into the central kabbalist icon, the Tree of Life, providing a continual link in the chain of tradition from the Ancient Hebrews through the joyous Renaissance kabbalists of Safed to contemporary mystics.

The ten sephirot (singular: *sephirah)* making up the Tree are a powerful meditative icon, a centering spiritual image, a path to find God in our lives on Earth. The *Hebrew Book of the Dead* is a call to consciousness and freedom. The Tree of Life offers us a disciplined, practical answer to that call.

Four Worlds - Ten Sephirot

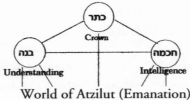

World of Atzilut (Emanation)

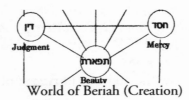

World of Beriah (Creation)

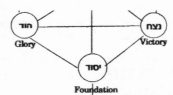

World of Yetzirah (Formation)

World of Assiyah (Action)

The Tree's roots are deep in the earth of this world. Its Crown is high in the heavens. Through the Tree of Life, God and the Worlds of Angels and Archangels are directly connected to this human World. The Tree is a column of light extending from the Kingdom to the Crown and beyond to the *Ayn Sof,* the Eternal, crossing all the Worlds.

What separates the Worlds is the רקיע, the *raki-a*.

And God said let there be a raki-a in the middle of the waters and let it divide the waters from the waters. And God made the raki-a and divided the waters which were under the raki-a from the waters which were above the raki-a. And God called the raki-a Heaven. (Gen. 1:6)

Ezekiel (1:22) saw the raki-a in his vision of the Chariot.
And over the heads of the living creatures there was the likeness of a raki-a, like the color of the terrible ice, stretched forth over their heads above.
Daniel (12:2,3) cites the *brightness of the raki-a.* In Exodus 24:10, the floor of Heaven is described as *clear and of sapphire stone* (Ex. 24:10)
The shaft of clear light extending from the Crown to the Kingdom is reflected and diffused through the medium of the *raki-a.* In ascending the Tree, we must cross this brightness, this terrible blue ice.

215

The Soul moves across two Worlds crossing the raki-a twice in its travels from life to life, born and reborn in an arc, an *arc-en-ciel*, a rainbow.

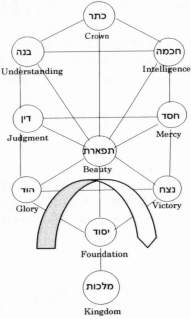

From its final place on Earth, in Assiyah, the World of Action, the human Soul rises to cross into the next world through the parted Sea of Ending, with "the water a wall on our right and our left." Beneath the sephirah Glory-of-God, the soul enters Yetzirah, the World of Formation. In glory we enter this *olam ha-bah,* this World to Come, triumphant, our bodies left behind on the distant shore.

Our journey on Earth is across the World of Assiyah in the Kingdom-of-God. Our concern is not with Yetzirah, the World to Come, but this very life and the demands we must meet while we walk in these bodies of mud. It is good to awaken, to remember the Worlds from which we came and to which we are returning. But our essential task is to live this life well. The Spirit of God has chosen to enter this place in which we find ourselves, this Temple, this holy habitation. The Tree of Life sustains us here and awakens us from our slumber, recalling us to our path.

This journey of the Tree is open to all. The Torah assures us that God is within each breath and each heartbeat and urges us to chose life that we may live in God. It is a universal path, unfolding alike for all conscious beings.

The image of our travels through the Worlds is a map of our own spiritual path through our lives. Our spiritual life on Earth, in the World of Assiyah, is a recapitulation of the journey of Asaph in the *Hebrew Book of the Dead*, of Joseph, the Dreamer.

Allegory of a different cave

There is a deep limestone cave in Africa where, hundreds of feet down labyrinthine dark passages, microbes blindly feed on manganese deposits and excrete sulfur. The sulfur they produce mixes with humid air from underground streams and forms sulphuric acid which drips on the rocky cave walls.

While dining on manganese, the microbes make holes in the walls, enlarging the cave. Below, the chemical burning of their sulphuric excrescence lowers the floor of the cave. Far from the light, this silent banquet enlarges and carves the cave.

Seen through an electron microscope, these microbes appear as spherical multitudes, each one a ball within whose cell wall is a living being. Each microbe moves, eats, excretes, and reproduces.

In its infinitesimal blindness, in its dim-witted munching of minerals, this microbe is at the front lines of Creation. Its spirit dances to the music of a distant Player.

Cannot the same be said of us? We are born, wet and flushed, drawing our first breath through brand new lungs. And from that instant until we release our last breath we cannot say we know where we are or what we are doing.

Nothing we see provides more than a passing perspective that, usually, proves false over time. Nothing explains cruelty, love, torture, and hatred. Nor the birth of children condemned to awful lives, nor animal slaughter, music, beauty, elephant tears and hurricanes. Through it all we just munch on. We can only be certain that we are and whatever we do is at the bidding of a Force of which we are an integral, creative part.

We breathe breath that is not ours. We are sustained each instant only by this continuous breath.

It is a continual Covenant.

Breathing alone, breathing this breath that is not me, assures me that I am here at the pleasure of Another, the Creator Whose-Breath-It-Is, the Ayn Sof, the Eternal

One. This realization is the first step of awareness. Simply knowing we live by the sufferance of Another is the first rung on the ladder leading out of Malchut, the first branch of the Tree leading to freedom.

Assiyah, this World of Action and Doing, is where we have gravity and gravitas, lox and bagels, Time, Space, bodies, nerves, and receptors plugged into the Source that sends us signals of light and sound and smell while playing our biochemistry like a harp in some celestial orchestra. For all our intellectual scope and kaleidoscopic emotions, we ride bodies that are biological machines of mud — earth, water and dissolved minerals, jerking about to the hum of electric currents buzzing down our neurons. Physically, we are greater than angels, less than a new car.

Welcome to the Earth World, Malchut, the Kingdom-of-God, the sole sephirah in Assiyah. Assiyah is both the Lowest of the Four Worlds and the most significant. Assiyah is the World down to which all Emanations flow from all the branches, leaves, and fruit of the Tree. The World whose Earthly roots feed the highest leaf on the Tree itself. Assiyah, in any event, is the World in which we find ourselves and whose meaning, by our own lights, we each try to figure out as we passage from infancy to old age, from birth to death.

There are religious and political systems in place that do much of the hard work of this calculation by fitting a template of order over the chaos of our days. And whether the order be true or false, it provides many of us with comfort along the way. Unfortunately, such systems also put us fast sleep and keep us comfortably drugged.

To find our way to God, we need to struggle to awaken and our first steps are here in Malchut.

Only here, in Malchut, the Kingdom-of-God, does a single sephirah occupy an entire World. The World of Assiyah. In the image of the Tree, all the Forces of Emanation and Creation and Formation lead to our actions in this Worldly Kingdom. We are a sum of sephirot and all our actions affect Creation itself. It is our work on Earth.

Finding God is not an idea but a process. An idea alone did not create the limestone Cave but the excrescence of a living biological system. Caves are not formed by geology alone but in partnership with biology. We are biologic Be-ings and it takes the work of all our being to stay awake in our quest for God.

When we set out to climb the sephirotic Tree, we need not be daunted by the impenetrability of Worlds, by the fragile, fetid nature of the human form. We breathe and thus, within ourselves, is the Holy Spirit of God. We act and thus are the sum of Creation. Here, we are both pitiful worms and lords of Creation.

When we are freed from this task and lifted up from the Pit to be carried across the Sea of Ending, for a time we will long for the sweetness of our lives in the World of Assiyah. But brooding above all, always, is the Ayn Sof.

Ayn Sof. Without End. The Eternal. The One from Whom all things flow. The utterly unknowable One.

We may not know the essence of the Ayn Sof, but it is possible to discern the Ways of God, the way the cave walls are eaten away, the track of God's passage in our days, in history, art, science, the movement of waves in the ocean and the formation of starry constellations. The hints our faulty senses and limited cognition provide are the only clues given us, directly. We have those and the continuing Covenant of the Breath. And beating of the heart, the drumming rhythm set in motion before we are born and turned off in concert with our final breath. Together, by witnessing the Ways of God outside our own cell wall and feeling the continual infusion of blood and breath within, we can gain a brief handhold on the branches of the Tree, a momentary respite from eating and producing.

For as the days of the Tree shall be the days of my people... Isaiah, 65:22

The Tree of Life is one mystical vision of the passage of the Ayn Sof through our days, one view of how the Ayn Sof flows through the Worlds.

We journey across this life, across time and space, our words, our actions creating joy and sorrow, wars and enterprises. We journey through the Realm of Malchut, a kingdom of confusion and chaos, for here we taste the fruit of the Tree of Knowledge and learn of separation and limitation.

In the center of the Garden grew the Tree of Life but we are forever drawn to the Tree of Knowledge of Good and Evil. We separate the fruit from the Tree. We eat and become Good and Evil. Thus too says the story of Asaph in the *Hebrew Book of the Dead.* In Malchut, the

221

dreamer filled with pride carries his birthright to the grave and beyond.

🔯 **Early kabbalists were fanatically devoted to the search for passageways to God**, ways to clear away the darkness and straighten the labyrinth. The World — this one and any others they encountered in their ecstasies and permutations, their prayers and dancing — is only an illusion that hides the face of God. Through the Tree of Life, these spiritual warriors challenged that illusion.

Putrid drop though we are, there burns within us God's will, spoken in our every breath and heartbeat. We contain the Holy Spirit.

In our search for God, it would help to know what these pious, devoted spiritual warriors knew. And if we can't follow most of their paths, and don't understand how many of their practices could work for them, what we can understand will help us gain another handhold in this free form climb up the Tree into consciousness. The Path of the Tree of Life is a ladder we may climb, step by step into the light, following the Word of God.

🔯 **Ages before the first kabbalists, the Ancient Hebrews knew the Tree.** The Tree of Life appears in the center of the Garden of Eden. In Exodus 25:31-37, there is a description of the Golden Menorah, the candlestick created for the desert sanctuary, the lights that were integral to the Temple service in Jerusalem. The menorah contains the central column and side columns of the Tree of Life, the ten almond blossoms of sephirot, the arms embracing four divisions of Worlds.

The Sefer Yetzirah — one of the most ancient of holy Ancient Hebrew writings — contains the detailed outline of the Tree and the sephirot.

If the Ancient Hebrews knew of this mystical Tree, then we should be able to find some passage through the Sephirot that reflects that central myth of their lives, the birth, death, and resurrection of Joseph, the stories found in the *Hebrew Book of the Dead*.

And we can. The passage of Asaph from his pit in Egypt across the split waters of the Sea of Ending into the desert wilderness follows the path of the Tree. The very names and influences of each sephirah in the Tree of Life play a role in Asaph's trials and triumphs. And our own.

Come and see.

At the base of the Tree of Life there is the Fourth World, the World of Assiyah, The World of Making and Doing. This is the World of Action with its single sephirah, *Malchut*, the Kingdom-of -God.

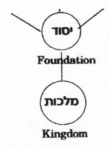

Above, illuminating the darkness, is the base of the Upper Worlds, *Yesod*, the Foundation-of-God, the source of Waters. Yesod is the Foundation of the Third World, a world that includes the sephirot *Hod,* Glory-of-God and *Netzah,* Victory-of-God. Together these three sephirot make up the World of Yetzirah, the World of Formation, the domain of Angels.

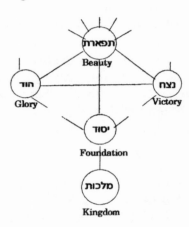

Yetzirah is the Water World, the container of the effluent flowing from the upper worlds. Through Yesod surge the power, energy and will of Creation for all sephirot empty into Foundation-of-God.

Yetzirah is ruled by a trinity of powers, two vice regents, Hod, Glory-of-God and Netzah, Victory-of-God, and the monarch, Yesod, Foundation-of-God.

Yesod, the generative center of all the Worlds, processes the male and female flows from the Upper Worlds and pours them into Malchut, the Kingdom-of-

God, in the receptive World of Assiyah. Malchut is frequently referred to as the Queen, the Shekkinah, the Female aspect of Creation, the Bride of God. Thus is the deeply sexual nature of living beings reflected in Tree. It is difficult, when visualizing dynamic action, to rely on the two-dimensional diagrammatic Tree.

Kabbalists have found many different forms to express this Tree.

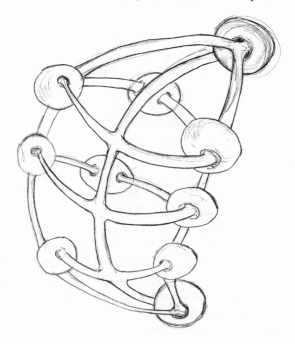

Visualizing a moving and dimensional Tree may help the seeker meditate on the cosmic motion of God's passage through the Worlds.

The Ancient Hebrews believed the raki-a separated the waters and the waters separated the Worlds. The word for Heaven in Hebrew is *sh'mayim* which means "Of waters."

To descend into this World of Action, it is necessary to cross the Waters separating the World of Formation from the World of Action. Those Waters of descent, the Jordan, or *yordayn* in Hebrew, separate for each of us in our time to be born.

To rise up from this World and enter the World of Yetzirah, we must first shed the Garment of the Body Only then may we cross the clear waters of the raki-a. In the *Hebrew Book of the Dead* the great waters of the Sea of Ending, standing between the World of Action and the World of Formation, separated for Asaph when it was his time to begin his trek across the Wilderness of Yetzirah.

There is great gladness crossing into Yetzirah. *The children of Israel walked upon dry land in the middle of the sea and the waters were a wall unto them on their right hand and on their left. (Ex. 14:29).* And when they found themselves delivered from bondage on the shores of the Wilderness they sang the triumphant Song of the Sea.

We cross the raki-a under the sephirah Hod, the Glory-of-God. We are home, closer to the source of light, freed of our appetites and physical compulsions, constrained by our memories.

We are headed for the Promised Land.

We are headed for Sinai.

Our first task is to become aware of where we are, aware of the present streaming moment, in order to free ourselves from the memories that weigh on us. Shed the vestiges of our bodies, our life in Assiyah, the mud that

226

clings to our Soul. Shed our appetites and fears, so we are
light and clear enough to cross the raki-a.

In the *Hebrew Book of the Dead,* the children of
Israel succumbed to memories during this part of their
wanderings. They whined, they lusted after meat, they
built a Golden Calf. As do we.

**Ascending from Malchut into the World of
Yetzirah** the soul of Asaph requires the Watery Gates of
the Kingdom to part. This water, the Yam Sof, is the Sea
of Ending, the gate that leads from the World of Assiyah
up to the World of Formation.

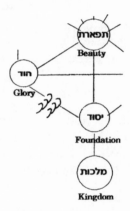

The soul of Asaph crosses into Yetzirah across the
split waters that reveal the earth below, the dry earth.
This is the same dry earth revealed in Genesis when God
says "Let the dry earth appear." On virgin soil, Asaph
crosses into the World of Yetzirah below the sephirah

Hod, the Glory-of-God. It is the soul's triumphant return to its Source, freedom from the dark floor of the cave.

High above the watery floor of the World of Yetzirah is the filtered brilliance of a distant Sun, the sephirah called Tiferet, Beauty-of-God. It is the central sephirah of Beriah, the World of Creation. Rotating above Tiferet, are the two Moons of this World, Judgment and Mercy, the sephirot of *Din* and *Chesed.*

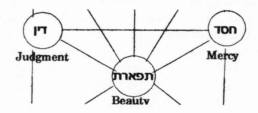

דין
Judgment

חסד
Mercy

תפארת
Beauty

Din, Judgment-of-God, is rigorous, principled, and implacable. Chesed, Mercy-of-God, is sweet and forgiving, loving and accepting. This is the vision of the Ancient Hebrews, adapted and shaped by the later kabbalists.

The first part of Asaph's journey across Yetzirah leads him to Teferith, the Beauty-of-God, the veiled but brilliant light shining over Yetzirah. Emerging from a triumphant march under the sephirah Glory-of-God, the Soul of Asaph now walks into the quadrant influenced by the cold distant moon of Din.

Here Asaph faces strict judgment of his life in Assiyah. This stage is preparation for *Teshuvah*, the Hebrew
word that means both "return" and "repentance."

At the Foot of Sinai, the slave to his physical appeti-
ties now lives on manna and follows a powerful Angel
across the wilderness. In this state of fear and confusion,
Asaph arrives at the foot of the Mountain that is called
Sinai, the worldly shadow of Tifereth whose base extends
to Foundation-of-God and thunderous crest is Keter, the
Crown-of-God.

In this most holy place, e sin of the Golden Calf
will complete the degradation of the Soul's life in its mud
body in Assiyah. It is here the Soul offers its body back to
its Creator in atonement. (See Bazak Thirty-three,
Strange Fire.) And it is from here that the journey continues.

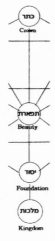

כתר
Crown

תפארת
Beauty

יסוד
Foundation

מלכות
Kingdom

Sinai, as a column of light through the Worlds

229

This Column of Light is nothing less than the center of the sephirotic Tree of Life.

At Sinai the soul of Asaph is torn between moving ahead and hanging back, between freedom and memory. In the soul's last worldly act, the Golden Calf is fashioned and the dance of death is danced. For this is the end of its life in darkness. It is here the Angel returns with the Tablets of Light and smashes them. It is here the soul eats the dust of the Golden Calf and waits in darkness until it can be purified, sanctified.

Crossing Yetzirah under the Influence of Mercy

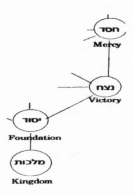

Once purified, the Soul moves on, but this time under a different quadrant. As the Soul travels East to the sephirah of Netzah, Victory-of-God, the full moon sephirah of Chesed, mercy and Lovingkindness-of-God lights the way in blessings .

Descending into the Kingdom-of-God means cross-ing the raki-a between the World of Yetzirah and the World of Assiyah. The Soul arrives at the Waters of De-scent, the wide and rocky stream, victorious in purifica-tion, sanctified. These waters, the Jordan, flow between Victory-of-God and the Foundation-of-God, between the sephirot Netzah and Yesod. The Soul enters back into life across the parted Waters of Descent.

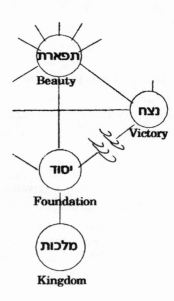

תפארת
Beauty

נצח
Victory

יסוד
Foundation

מלכות
Kingdom

The Soul returns to the Kingdom-of-God to do the work of the Lord. In a fresh body, trailing clouds of glory, with burgeoning appetites, it will grow and eat, reproduce and compost this mighty cave into a Temple in the service of YHVH.

231

This being can choose to do its work in peace and joy, part of the continuing work of Creation, God's breath and heartbeat a constant reminder of home.

There are higher worlds in the writings of the Ancient Hebrew and in the Tree of Life. The Angel Mosheh does not descend across the Jordan but, like Enoch and the Prophet Elijah, rises from the top of the mountain into Beriah, the World of Creation. We do not know the furthest reaches of the human soul but can only work in love and faith, in joy and hope, to ascend the Tree of Life in the course of our days on Earth.

All we have, all we can ever have, is the option to cling to God. Devka-Bo. We can recognize our own God self as part of the Ayn Sof, the unending being of us, and cherish the power and glory of a victorious life in God.

A Prayer. I have kept you always before my eyes. The Tree of Life unfolds before me and before I fall asleep in the grinding of my days, let me remember. Soon, soon I will be lifted up and taken across the wilderness of Yetzirah. Soon, I will be home. Praise, all praise to God!

Glossary

Acharai	After (time); back (structure).
Ad-tohm	Make whole.
Aron	Ark, cabinet.
Asaph	Carried Off; the biblical Joseph.
Assiyah	World of Action, the World of Making, World of Doing.
Atzilut	The World of Emanation, the World closest to the Ayn Sof.
Ayn Sof	The Eternal; literally, without end.
Aysh Zerah	Strange fire.
Aytz	A tree.
Aytzmot	Skeleton. (Literally, Tree of Death).
Bamidbar	In the wilderness. The biblical Book of Numbers.
Bazak	Epiphany. (Literally, lightning flash)
Bereshith	"In the beginning"; The biblical Book of Genesis.
Beriah	The World of Creation.
Chesed	Lovingkindness, a sephirah.
Chofesh	Freedom.
Devar	Word; thing.
Devarim	"Words"; biblical Book of Deuteronomy.
Devekuth	Intimate attachment to God.
Din	Judgment, A sephirah. Also: *gevurah*.

Gematriya	A system through which meaning is derived from words by means of the numerical value of the consonants.
Gevurah	Strength, Power, a sephirah. Also: *din.*
Kabbalah	Receive; A variety of systems and approaches leading to mystical, direct knowledge of God.
Karov	Near; the root "sacrifice."
Makom	Place. Used as referent for the unapproachable, the unknowable locus of divinity.
Malchut	Kingdom, a sephirah.
Mavet	Death.
Mezzuzah	Doorpost.
Me'od	Very.
Midrash	Interpretation of Scripture, search.
Mishkan	Desert tabernacle.
Mishpatim	Ordinance, judgments.
Mitzrayim	From *tzur*, narrow, painful; Used to refer to ancient Egypt.
Mosheh	(n.) Moses (v.) Bear, rescue..
Nefesh	Being, the individual Soul portion; from *nafash*, to rest. For some, the Animal-Soul
Neshamah	The God-Soul (See Bazak Three).
Nikrat Tzur	Cleft of the rock.
Pay, P'nei	Face (human); before (time).
Pesachti	I shall pass over; Root of Passover.
Peshat	The simple, direct meaning of a text.
Ruach	Spirit, Wind. Soul portion (See Bazak Three)

Sephirah	Count, number; construct for the emanation of YHVH's powers through the Worlds.
Shekkinah	YHVH's presence on Earth; the feminine.
Shemot	"Names"; biblical Book of Exodus. (When divided, *sh'* and *mot* mean "of death.")
Sneh	The burning bush.
Sof	End, ending.
Tiferet	Beauty, a sephirah.
Vayikra	"And then He called"; the biblical Book of Leviticus.
Yam	Sea.
Yavashar	Virgin soil, dry land.
Yeridah	Descend, descent. The Jordan River leading from Yetzirah to the Promised Land takes its name from this word.
Yetzirah	The World of Formation, the World of Spirit beyond this World of Assiyah. The setting for the wilderness.
Yi'hi Or	Be light

The Hebrew Book of the Dead

THE HEBREW BOOK OF THE DEAD
In the Wilderness

Scriptural References

Genesis

1:9,10	**Bazak Two** Water
2:3,6,7; 1:27	**Bazak Three** A Living Soul
28:12-15	**Bazak Nine** Behold, a Ladder
37:15-20	**Bazak Thirteen** The Pit
50:24-26	**Bazak Seventeen** A Tree of Death

Exodus

3:13-15	**Bazak Twenty-One** The Name

Leviticus

9:24, 10:1-3	**Bazak Thirty-Three** Strange Fire

Deuteronomy

30:11-14	**Bazak Thirty-Nine** The Word
30:19, 20	**Bazak Forty** Choose Life

Joshua

3:11, 3:17, 4:19	**Bazak Forty-Two** The Covenant
24:32	**Bazak Forty-Four** In an Open Field